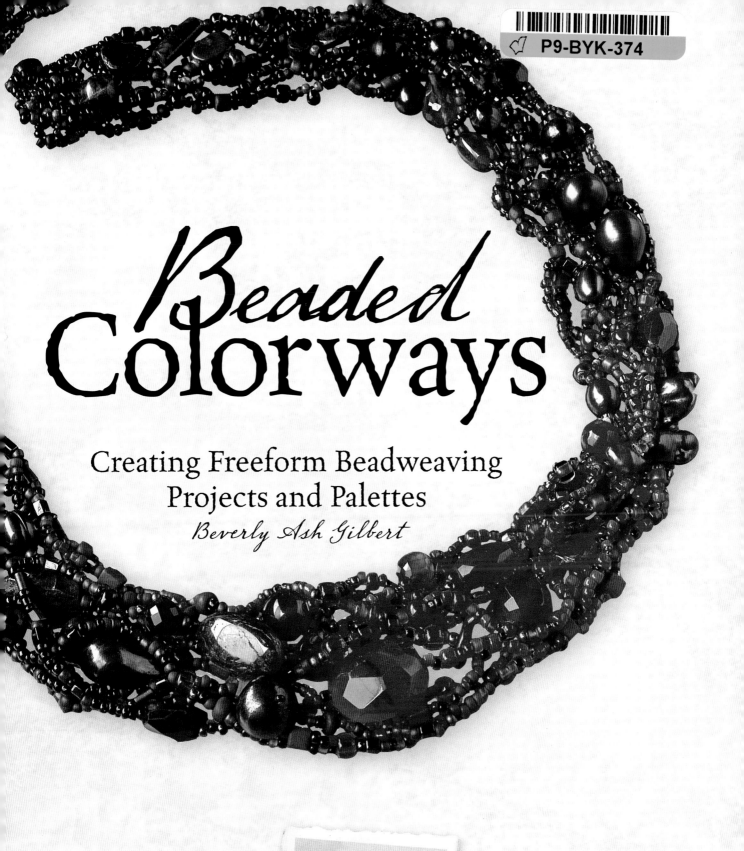

Beaded Colorways

Creating Freeform Beadweaving Projects and Palettes

Beverly Ash Gilbert

NORTH LIGHT BOOKS

Cincinnati, Ohio

www.mycraftivity.com

13 12 11 10   5 4 3 2

Distributed in Canada by Fraser Direct
100 Armstrong Avenue
Georgetown, ON, Canada L7G 5S4
Tel: (905) 877-4411

Distributed in the U.K. and Europe by David & Charles
Brunel House, Newton Abbot, Devon, TQ12 4PU, England
Tel: (+44) 1626 323200, Fax: (+44) 1626 323319
E-mail: postmaster@davidandcharles.co.uk

Distributed in Australia by Capricorn Link
P.O. Box 704, S. Windsor, NSW 2756 Australia
Tel: (02) 4577-3555

Library of Congress Cataloging-in-Publication Data
Ash Gilbert, Beverly.
  Beaded colorways : creating freeform beadweaving projects and palettes / by Beverly Ash Gilbert.
      p. cm.
  Includes index.
  ISBN 978-1-60061-318-0 (pbk. : alk. paper)
  1. Beadwork. 2. Jewelry making. I. Title.
  TT860.A745 2009
  745.594'2--dc22

                    2009024618

Editor: Julie Hollyday

Designer: Geoff Raker

Production Coordinator: Greg Nock

Photographers: Christine Polomsky, David Peterson

Photo Stylist: Lauren Emmerling

All color wheel relationship illustration images: created by Joie Moring (Moring Design) and Beverly Ash Gilbert

Portrait photo: Diane Ahern (www.dianeahern.com)

Nebula photo and Ice photo: www.dreamstime.com

All other inspiration photographs: Beverly Ash Gilbert

fw
media
www.fwmedia.com

Metric Conversion Chart

to convert	to	multiply by
Inches	Centimeters	2.54
Centimeters	Inches	0.4
Feet	Centimeters	30.5
Centimeters	Feet	0.03
Yards	Meters	0.9
Meters	Yards	1.1
Sq. Inches	Sq. Centimeters	6.45
Sq. Centimeters	Sq. Inches	0.16
Sq. Feet	Sq. Meters	0.09
Sq. Meters	Sq. Feet	10.8
Sq. Yards	Sq. Meters	0.8
Sq. Meters	Sq. Yards	1.2
Pounds	Kilograms	0.45
Kilograms	Pounds	2.2
Ounces	Grams	28.3
Grams	Ounces	0.035

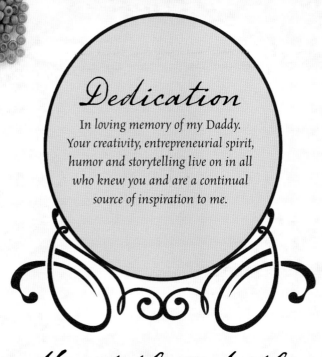

Dedication

In loving memory of my Daddy.
Your creativity, entrepreneurial spirit,
humor and storytelling live on in all
who knew you and are a continual
source of inspiration to me.

About the Author

Beverly Ash Gilbert is a self-taught artist who believes that anything is possible. She believes there is an artist in all of us just waiting for the inspiration, the right medium and positive encouragement along the way in order to blossom. She believes changes in direction, following your dreams and jumping up in the morning bursting with creativity and ideas and excitement about your work is what life is all about.

She loves playing with color and pushing the boundaries of her creativity—sometimes finding new paths to follow, sometimes tripping over her own feet, but always learning. She thrives on sharing what she has learned and helping students blast through their own creative boundaries.

She travels around the country teaching but has her roots firmly planted in the Pacific Northwest surrounded by three creative men—her husband, Jerry, and two sons, Morgan and Brandon—and lots of color!

Beverly loves walking on the beach, wine with friends, spontaneous backyard picnics with neighbors, chocolate, happy people, good books and cozy fires, snuggling with her boys, listening to her husband play guitar, gathering flowers from her garden, family movie night with Jerry's homemade pizza, her macro lens, laughing, and playing with color and beads.

Acknowledgements

How can I thank you, dear family and friends, for your inspiration, encouragement, support and understanding as I dove head first into this creative journey? You have stood by me through long hours, tears, laughter, not enough time together and my obsession with beads and color.

Joie Moring: Thank you for the countless hours immersed in color wheels, color relationships, chocolate, soup and laughter. You are a dear friend and a continual source of inspiration. You have taken my dreams and helped me fly, and oh, what an eye for color you have!

Susan Reynolds Leonhardt: I owe this all to your nudge down a path that has given me so much purpose, inspiration and direction in my life. Who would have thought on that January day in 2002 that we would be walking (or running!) down the paths we are now on?

Terry Voss, Sherri Lynn, Mariangela Gibson, Tracy Hamblin McPhee, Anne Ryan and Marianne Foster: You all are always there with positive encouragement, humor and a big shoulder. Thank you for understanding when I need it most, for sending warm thoughts from afar and sharing conversation, wine, coffee and hugs.

Diane Ahern, Dagmar Fleuren and Kenda Gaynham: Thank for your creative inspiration from behind a lens. Diane, thank you for taking my portrait and convincing me that wrinkles are elegant and wise and we've earned them (just so we don't zoom in too close!). Dagmar and Kenda: Thanks for your senses of color, proportion and composition mixed with a heavy doses of friendship from the other side of the world.

Jacqueline Talarico and Marcy McKenzie, who wander beaches from Prince Edward Island to Texas and send me beautiful treasures to share with students.

Mom, Aunt Carolyn and fond memories of Grandma Grimm, who introduced me to, and inspired me with, color.

Tonia Davenport, who asked me to write this book, then patiently and gracefully pulled it out of me!

Julie Hollyday, who stood by my vision and—along with Christine Polomsky, Geoff Raker and the wonderfully creative team at North Light Books—took my ramblings, projects, color wheels, soups and inspirations and worked their colorful magic!

And especially my husband, Jerry, and sons, Morgan and Brandon—thank you for your patience while I holed up in my corner to write and bead. Brandon, your smiles, hugs, shoulder massages and help making bead soup are so much more cherished than you will ever know. Morgan, you are a wonderful artist and story teller and I am so proud of you! And Jerry, I am continually inspired by your creativity, strength, determination and ability to do anything. Without your example, I would never have had the confidence to push forward. You are truly my Renaissance man!

Contents

Introduction

I am like you. I have an artist inside yearning to create, to play with color and texture and form, to make something with my hands that I feel proud of, that others want to look at and touch. The child in me wants to break a few rules and branch off onto my own creative path.

Yet how many times do we lack the confidence to push forward, experiment, and lay open our work for others to see? In fact, the artist inside is often fragile—and we are our biggest critic.

Working with color and experimenting with freeform style can be a little daunting, even scary at first: Where do I start? What is it going to look like? Will I like it? What will others think? This book is about throwing away the rules, wandering down our own paths and building confidence along the way. Because unlike set color combinations and patterned work, freeform beadweaving is undefined—there is no right or wrong way to do it.

The course is wide open and changes direction as you go—I think of it like meandering through a meadow, leaping over tall grasses, skirting a big puddle, being distracted by a bird's nest, flower, or little creature and wandering over to take a closer look. Freeform beadweaving is joyful, freeing and stimulating; and once you learn the basics, no longer intimidating—it is actually quite easy to learn! Best of all, it enables you to forge your own trails and really play with color.

I am drawn to color, motivated by color, energized and excited by color. I marvel how a single hue can be given depth by including shadows and highlights and how different colors play against each other. Sure, I have a few favorite combinations that keep calling me, but I am thrilled when I push myself in new directions. I am always learning how to use color and being inspired by what I see around me.

Beads are a fabulous medium for experimenting with color, and the enormous range of colors found in seed beads is exhilarating! By following along with me as I work with color and create seed bead soups, you will learn how to build palettes with depth and movement. This book is not about giving you specific colors to work with—color is too personal for that—it is about helping you build confidence in your own ability to pull together palettes that energize you and make you feel good. Then, ultimately, you will use your gorgeous mixes in fun and beautiful ways.

The discussions and projects in this book build on each other, getting more involved—but not necessarily more difficult—as you move from project to project. Within each section are a handful of projects, and though it isn't necessary to do every one in order to learn the techniques needed to move on, in many cases, reviewing them will be helpful.

This book will show you how to work with color, freeform beadweaving and even basic metalworking so you can expand your own creative style. My hope is to inspire you, to help spark new ideas and to stimulate the artist inside of you to find your own unique path and your creative expression in color and texture. So for all of you who love color and want to explore ways to use it in your beadwork, come with me on this journey to see where it will take you and what wonderful paths you will create!

Color Theory & Beadweaving Basics

So many of us are drawn to beads and jewelry making because of the vast array of colors and color combinations that are possible; many of us are intrigued with gardening and fabrics and home décor for the same reason!

I want to share some of the insights and techniques I have learned on my journey with color and beads that you can add to your repertoire. Working with color is natural for some and a little more challenging for others, but all of us can gain color confidence by understanding the language of color, drawing on powerful tools, surrounding ourselves with colors that make us feel good and working along with each other. Observing color—really seeing what's around you: the beauty in nature, the patterns in fabric, the colors other artists pull together—is one of the most important first steps. Getting in close to see the nuances of colors, like the shadows and highlights on a blade of grass, helps us to understand why color is so powerful and ultimately how to use it successfully.

The first part of this chapter will give you insight and tools for enhancing how you work with color and walk you through using the color wheels at the back of the book. We will use these tools to create colorful mixes of beads called bead soups! I will show you how I make monochromatic bead soups that are beautiful on their own, then walk you through making your own unique multicolor mixes filled with depth and movement—don't be surprised if friends ask for handfuls to display in their homes!

The second part of this chapter is focused on beadweaving techniques. I have included basic Netting and Peyote stitches along with some handy hints and tips to give you a solid understanding of basic beadweaving stitches before we throw away the rules in the freeform projects later in the book.

So have fun; surround yourself with colorful inspirations, beads and your new color wheels; and get ready to create beautiful palettes with color and beads!

Working with color is exhilarating! But how do you create movement and depth in your own color palettes, and where do you look for inspiration? Before you pull out tubes of beads (or paint or bolts of fabric), it is helpful to understand the language of color and employ tools to help you mix different colors together.

Emotional Response to Color

Color surrounds us, influences us and evokes emotions—when we are surrounded by colors we love, we feel energized, creative, peaceful and happy. However, when we walk into a room full of color we don't like, we feel uncomfortable, stifled and more critical. Why is it that people respond differently to colors, and why do some people absolutely love colors that others don't like at all?

There are many factors that influence how we perceive and react to color. Past experiences are important. Perhaps you remember eating cookies and drinking lemonade in Grandma's cool blue sunporch with white gauzy curtains billowing in the breeze. Or maybe you have cozy memories of spending time with family in a dark wood cabin with a blazing fire and red-and-orange plaid blankets around your shoulders? These color combinations will spark good feelings. Someone else, however, may see the same colors and relive a bad memory. Also, each of the colors by itself may not be as influential as the combination: Is it the cool blue walls or the way the diffused sunlight plays across them that is so vivid in your mind?

Of course, fads can have powerful influences on our color choices. Advertisers spend lots of money seducing us into the newest color craze so we are anxious to repaint, redecorate, retile and buy new clothes, makeup and even cars.

Regardless of our color experiences or the latest fads, if we look good in a color, it makes us feel good, and that naturally translates to how we perceive that color. Do you remember the 1980s book *Color Me Beautiful*? I still have a tattered copy that I refer to and drag with me to show students because it really works. Not all of us correspond precisely to any one generic "season," but when you look at each color palette, you will naturally be drawn to the colors that best describe you. Despite any current fad, these are the colors that you look good in and, when you wear them, you feel good in. How wonderful when fads correspond to your colors!

For me, the "autumn palette" of brown, teal, chartreuse, orange, copper and bronze is my favorite and I have filled my closet and my home with these colors, which are all colors I look good in. Years ago, the "summer palette" of mauve and dusty blue was all the rage, and my friend Kathy, with her blond hair, blue eyes and rosy skin, looked great in them. However, I looked terrible—kind of a sick shade of yellow!

If you don't like the latest home or fashion palette, don't worry, it will pass and just around the corner will be another set of "must have" colors. My suggestion is to use these fads for one of many sources of inspiration but to ultimately follow your own sense of color.

Inspiration in Nature

A single color, no matter how much you love it, never has as much power as when it is used in combination with other colors and textures. Even within a single color family, we crave highlights, shades and textural variations to imbue depth and intrigue. Leaves, the ocean, a sunset, sand, terra-cotta tiles, a hydrangea blossom—their beauty lies in the color and textural variations.

Hydrangea leaves

These variations can be subtle or dramatic, but solid color blocks are rarely seen in nature (and only if you observe a small enough sample). If you fell in love with "leaf green" and tried to recreate it, you would be hard pressed to do so with one tube of paint or one tube of beads. Look at the hydrangea leaves and count how many colors of green you see—are there five or ten or more? Note the deep shadows; the shiny leaves that reflect a little blue from the sky; the new, bright yellow–green leaves with their stems, veins and serrated edges. It is this complexity that gives leaves movement, depth and life. No wonder artists look to nature for inspiration in color as well as subject.

I am driven by color. I will buy a book, a pillow, a scarf or anything if the colors leap out at me. Conversely, I can be turned away from a fabulous art technique because the colors the artist used don't speak to me. Sometimes, this is a difference in taste, but often, the palette seems flat to me and needs a little tweak to give it movement and depth. However, if my eye is stimulated, then even palettes that I wouldn't normally work with seem beautiful.

Language of Color

Whether you are already confident in working with color or a little intimidated, it is important to be able to define each color you see in terms of its color family, saturation and value. This will not only help you place the color on the color wheel, but it will also enable you to relay information to others.

What Color is it?

"A rose by any other name… is just a rose" or is it salmon, coral, pink or fuchsia? As seductive as these names are, for they inspire wonderful images, they don't convey the same color to all people. Was that "salmon" King Salmon or Coho, fresh, baked or smoked?

Defining the color family (also called hue) is the first step. My mother introduced me to color by using the old Crayola color boxes. The colors were named by their parents: remember orange red and blue green? These names tell us exactly what colors were mixed together to make the new color.

Perhaps it would even be easier to visualize if we said orange + red (orange with a little bit of red), red-orange (an equal mix of red and orange) and red + orange (red with a little bit of orange). Therefore, pink + orange tells us that it is a tint of red (add white) with a small amount of orange. Not as sumptuous as "salmon," but easier to define.

So how do you know if your color is orange + red or red + orange? A color on its own may be difficult to analyze. But place it next to a similar color, and you will be able to tell whether it leans toward or away from the other color, as seen in the progression from orange to red in photo 1.

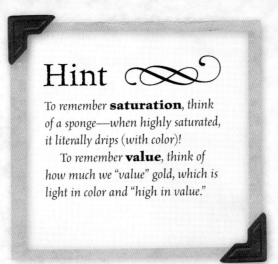

Hint

To remember **saturation**, think of a sponge—when highly saturated, it literally drips (with color)!

To remember **value**, think of how much we "value" gold, which is light in color and "high in value."

Is it Saturated?

Saturation is a measure of how pure, bright or intense a color is. The more intense the color, the higher the saturation. If anything is added to the pure color, it loses saturation. For instance on the color strip in photo 2, when black is added to red-orange, the color becomes less saturated (don't confuse saturation with how dark it is—this will be discussed later). Similarly, when white is added to the red-orange, it becomes less saturated. A color can be de-saturated by adding a bit of its complement (see page 14) to achieve an earthy, brown version of the same color. For instance, terra-cotta can be created by adding a small amount of blue-green into red-orange as seen in the inner rings of the color wheel on page 12.

What Value is it?

Another important attribute is the darkness or lightness of a color, known as "value." The lighter the color, the higher the value; conversely, the darker the color, the lower the value. When you are looking at colors from a single color family, the relative value is easy to determine. However, it is a little harder when comparing value from different color families—the color gets in the way! The easiest way to determine value is to squint your eyes so very little light hits the cones in your eyes (the color sensors). Now compare the lightness or darkness you see with the gray scale in photo 3. It may be tough at first, but with practice you will become pretty good at determining the relative value.

Photo 1: Color families from orange to red

Add Black   Saturated   Add White

Photo 2: The red-orange color family with various saturations

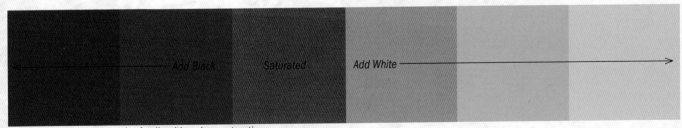

Photo 3: Grayscale

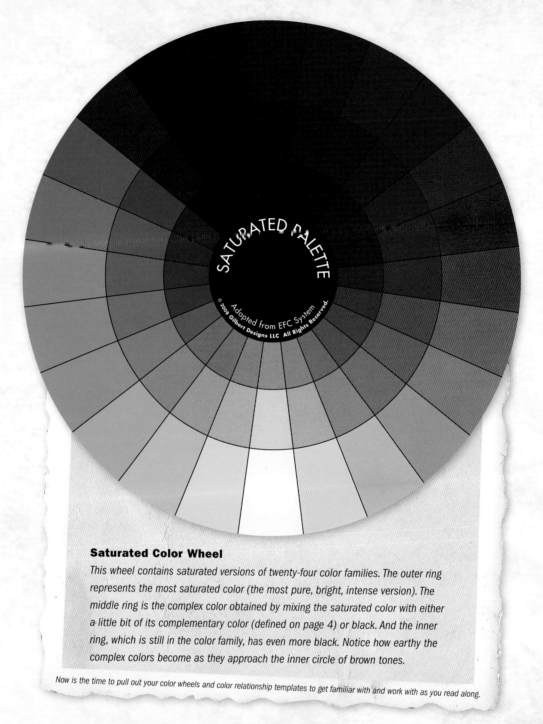

Saturated Color Wheel

This wheel contains saturated versions of twenty-four color families. The outer ring represents the most saturated color (the most pure, bright, intense version). The middle ring is the complex color obtained by mixing the saturated color with either a little bit of its complementary color (defined on page 4) or black. And the inner ring, which is still in the color family, has even more black. Notice how earthy the complex colors become as they approach the inner circle of brown tones.

Now is the time to pull out your color wheels and color relationship templates to get familiar with and work with as you read along.

Color Wheel

Are you an expert at defining color yet? Some people can analyze a color all by itself and retain a memory of its nuance. My Aunt Carolyn has this gift. I made a bedspread in antiqued shades of beige, teal (blue + green) and burgundy (red + violet). Carolyn saw it on one of her visits and six months later sent me a swatch of material for a pillow in the exact shade of the deep red + violet roses. Her eye for color is amazing. But for the rest of us, a cheat sheet comes in handy: the color wheel!

I think the color wheel is the most valuable tool for working with color. And no matter how many palettes I create, I always pull it out to help me enhance the depth and movement of the colors.

Moses Harris first created the color wheel in 1766 and defined the primary colors of red, yellow and blue from which all other colors could be made. The secondary colors are made from combinations of the primary colors: orange, green and violet (or purple), and the tertiary colors are the colors made from combining primary and secondary colors: orange-red, red-orange, etc. His color wheel system delineated eighteen separate color families arranged as pieces of a pie in a large circle.

Currently, many color wheels on the market contain only twelve divisions of color. Computer monitors, on the other hand, will break the colors into so many pieces that it is almost overwhelming. However, the number of divisions you have available in your color wheel is not as important as being able to accurately describe your color and visualize the possible combinations. Because I love the complex colors between the main divisions, I find twelve divisions are too few, so I divided the color wheel included in this book into twenty-four color families.

You'll find two color wheels attached to the back cover of the book. One color wheel is a relatively saturated one, with "shades" of the saturated color (darkened with black) in the inner rings of the wheel. The second wheel is

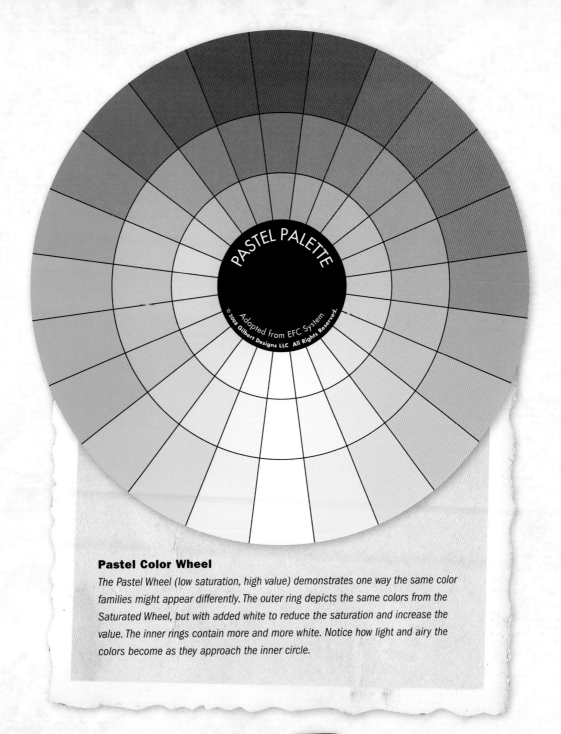

Pastel Color Wheel

The Pastel Wheel (low saturation, high value) demonstrates one way the same color families might appear differently. The outer ring depicts the same colors from the Saturated Wheel, but with added white to reduce the saturation and increase the value. The inner rings contain more and more white. Notice how light and airy the colors become as they approach the inner circle.

a pastel wheel (low saturation, high value) which shows "tints" (lightened with white) of the same color families. Flip both wheels over to read the color family names associated with each of the twenty-four color segments.

Not all colors you use will fall onto a specific swatch of color on the two wheels—some will be higher or lower in saturation, lighter or darker in value or "muddied" by additional grey or brown tones. However, once you train your eye to see color families, you will be able to place all colors on your wheels even with these differences.

The following information and the color wheel examples throughout this book will help you train your eye to see and use color more confidently. Pull out your color wheels and compare them to the colors all around you. With practice, you will be able to determine what color family your color is closest to, even if it is saturated, muddied or lighter or darker.

Hint ∽

Colors on the same ring of the color wheel look yummy together, like this wheel showing only the colors on the middle ring of the Pastel Color Wheel. This is because they have a lot in common—they are all of the same value and saturation. This is a key observation and will come in handy later on!

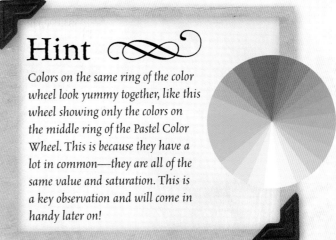

Exploring Color Relationships

Once you have defined your color, you are ready to start combining it with other colors in an endless array of possibilities. Interestingly, some of the most pleasing color combinations fall within a defined set of relationships. This is not to say you can't create gorgeous color ensembles with non-traditional relationships: Jinny Beyer (see Favorite Books in Resources on page 126) maintains that any colors can be used together as long as the transitional elements are present. I agree!

However, the traditional combos are a good place to start. Without getting too technical, the traditional combinations are based on mathematics, and the ones people use most frequently are included in your templates.

The templates in this book include all of the following color relationships, with some combined on one wheel. For instance, on the Split Complementary/Expanded Split Complementary template, the single split is denoted by the arrows within the expanded window. The Expanded Triad template also includes arrows that highlight the simple triad. Gorgeous combinations can be achieved by going beyond the popular complementary relationships. Therefore, on the Analogous template, a complementary color family is also included. The Expanded Complementary template shows the complement can be as narrow or wide as you like.

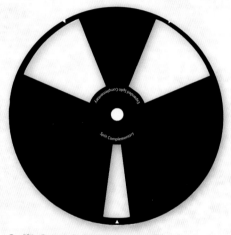

Complementary
One of the most popular of all relationships, this one includes colors that lie opposite to each other on the color wheel

Analogous
Colors that sit next to each other on the color wheel (choose as big a slice of pie as you want!)

Expanded Complementary
Analogous colors with a bit of a complementary color

Split Complementary (denoted by white arrows)
A color and the two colors that lay on either side of its complement

Expanded Split Complementary
Split complementary with a wider array of colors

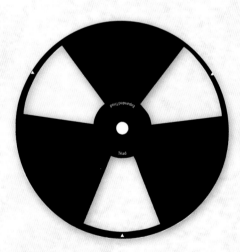

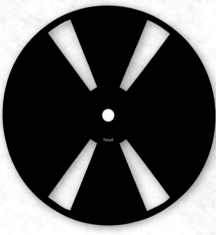

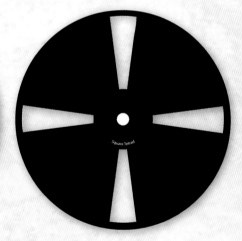

Triad (denoted by white arrows)
Three colors equidistant on the color wheel

Expanded Triad
Expand the triad to include more color families

Tetrad
Two sets of complementary colors offset from a central complementary pair

Square Tetrad
Two sets of complementary colors offset at right angles from each other

Using the Color Wheel

Here are some examples to help you become familiar with using your color wheel and templates. To begin, you need to choose a color. For this example, I chose a color at random to see what possible combinations I could make. When choosing your own colors, sometimes it's hard to know what color to start with—do you have a favorite color? Or a new color that intrigues you? Is there an existing color in your design you would like to work with in a new way?

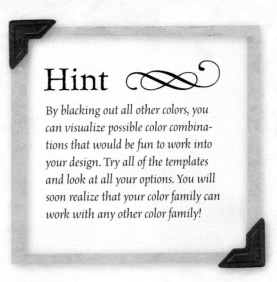

Hint ✦

By blacking out all other colors, you can visualize possible color combinations that would be fun to work into your design. Try all of the templates and look at all your options. You will soon realize that your color family can work with any other color family!

Defining color

Once you have a color in mind, it helps to define it. To do this, place the color next to the wheel to try to find the closest match. Don't worry if it is lighter or darker, less saturated or duller than the colors you see, it will still fall into a family. Now describe it as closely as possible.

In this example, I see that I have a saturated yellow + green. Now I can start combining it with other colors. In fact, knowing where a color comes from is important in the process of determining where you want it to go and what colors you want to combine with it.

Discovering combinations

Now comes the exciting part! To see what combinations are possible with your color, place any template over the wheel so that it shows in an open window. I randomly chose the Split Complementary template and spun it so the yellow + green color family is showing. The red + violet and blue green beads of similar saturation make a stunning combination.

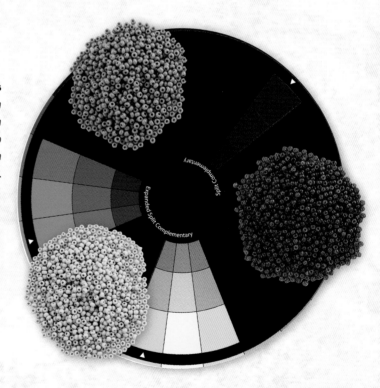

Hint ✦

An earthy, rich combination can be achieved by using the same color families, but with lower saturation, as seen in the inner rings of the color wheel.

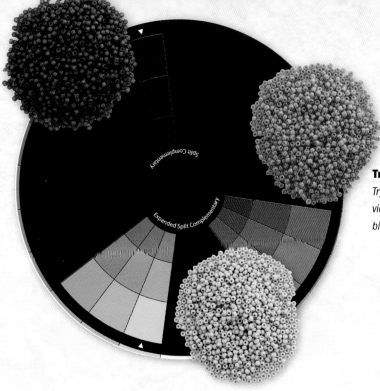

Trying more combinations

Try spinning the template to reveal different options. By centering it on the violet + blue color family, the yellow + green is still visible, but now in combination with the orange for an equally stunning combination of colors.

Another combination

Spin the template once more and another color combination is revealed. There are so many ways to use a color, and these examples used only one template! By trying other templates, you will be able to combine your color with any other color you want to use.

Choosing relationships

If you start with more than one color, all the easier—now all you have to do is determine how they are related. Try one template at a time and spin the wheel to find their various relationships. For instance, blue and red can work together in a tetrad, an expanded triad or an expanded split complementary relationship. Choose one of these relationships and add other colors to make the palette pop.

Don't Forget Saturation and Value

In the previous exercises, I chose colors close in saturation (intensity and purity) and value (lightness or darkness). This wasn't by accident. Yes, it is possible to work with any two colors, and I encourage you to do so, but it is important to understand that our eyes move more smoothly between colors that are similar in some attribute, whether it be family, saturation or value. This is because our eyes are stimulated by areas of high contrast. If this contrast is in just one of the color attributes, then the result can be stunning (just look at van Gogh's gorgeous color pal-ettes). However, if the contrast is in more than one attribute—such as far away from each other in color family and of different saturation and/or value—the result will be jarring and uncomfortable. This is not to say that you need to be comfortable: you can create a lot of drama with highly contrasting colors. But if you want more harmony, being conscious of all of the color's attributes will enable you to get the results you want.

This concept is shown in the bead soup created with gems below.

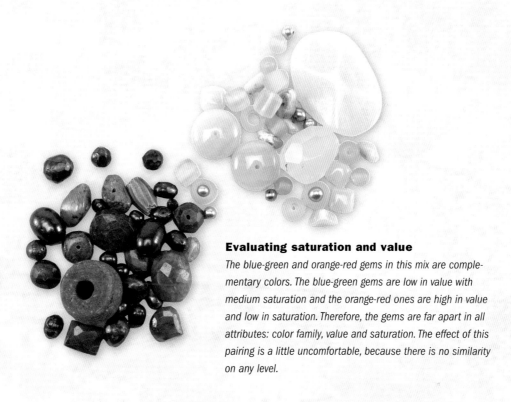

Evaluating saturation and value

The blue-green and orange-red gems in this mix are complementary colors. The blue-green gems are low in value with medium saturation and the orange-red ones are high in value and low in saturation. Therefore, the gems are far apart in all attributes: color family, value and saturation. The effect of this pairing is a little uncomfortable, because there is no similarity on any level.

These color strips correspond to the wedges on both the Saturated and Pastel Color Wheels showing the two complementary color families, expanded from high to low value, and are the closest match to the gems above.

Providing transitions

Adding some more blue-green gems, which are low in saturation and high in value (similar to the original orange-red ones), will provide a transition between the two original piles and enable the eye to move more smoothly over the entire mix.

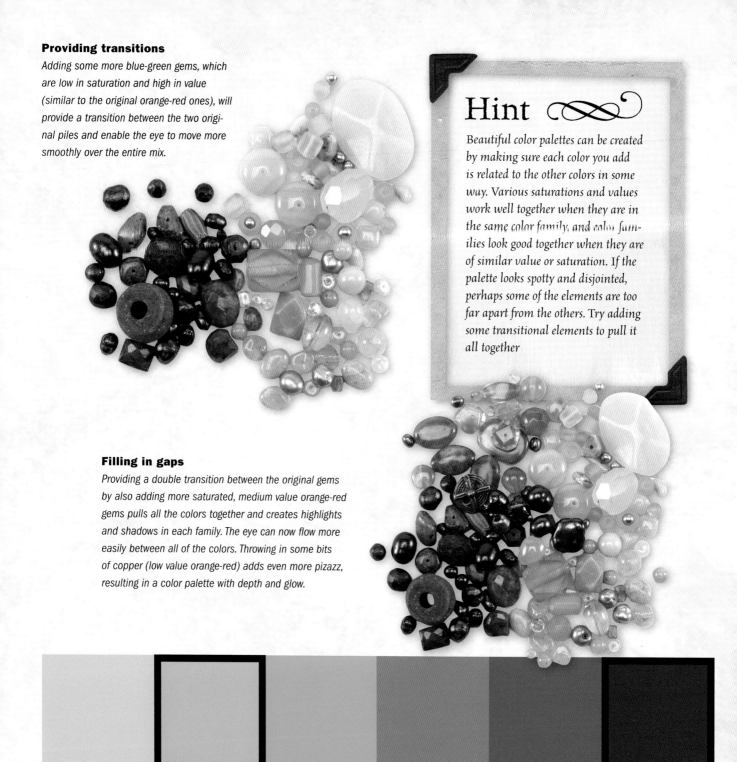

Hint

Beautiful color palettes can be created by making sure each color you add is related to the other colors in some way. Various saturations and values work well together when they are in the same color family, and color families look good together when they are of similar value or saturation. If the palette looks spotty and disjointed, perhaps some of the elements are too far apart from the others. Try adding some transitional elements to pull it all together

Filling in gaps

Providing a double transition between the original gems by also adding more saturated, medium value orange-red gems pulls all the colors together and creates highlights and shadows in each family. The eye can now flow more easily between all of the colors. Throwing in some bits of copper (low value orange-red) adds even more pizazz, resulting in a color palette with depth and glow.

The above transitions are seen in these color strips. The additional gems are closer in value and saturation, allowing the soup to blend together more easily. As shown on the strips, a variety of values and saturation levels are used for each color family so the eye can move more easily from one color to another.

Just as a painter uses many tubes of paint, the most dramatic and visually stimulating beadwork is created with bead soups. With a mix of beads, you can incorporate shadows, highlights and subtle or dramatic color variations even within a monochromatic scheme.

At their core, bead soups are made up of seed beads of all sizes, shapes and finishes. Larger beads and gems can be added for a visual punch. But beyond the raw materials, bead soups allow you to create color palettes that are sure to inspire you. The more colors and textures you incorporate into the bead soup, the more depth and movement you will achieve in your palette. For textural impact, it is important to include all seed bead sizes (from 15/0 to 5/0), shapes and finishes (matte, shiny, iridescent, etc.) for each color in your palette. I have been known to draw from over fifty different seed bead types to create a single soup!

Where do I Start?

This is a hard question for those of us who love color. In fact, I usually spend a ridiculous amount of time trying to decide what colors I want to work with—there are so many scrumptious choices!

When I create bead soups just for the sake of mixing color, I try to push myself into colors I don't normally use. But when I am mixing colors to use in a specific project, then I am more choosy—I want to make sure I will love it and wear it! So perhaps I will pull out an outfit in dire need of a set of earrings. Or I sort through photos, either ones I've taken myself or that I've collected from books and magazines, for inspiration. I also grab my color wheel and zero in on a color or color combination that jumps out at me.

It all starts with a monochromatic color scheme. Monochromatic, however, doesn't mean boring. In fact, no matter how many color families I end up using in my palette, I always create monochromatic bead soups for each before I mix them together. This is the best way to make sure I have shadows and highlights that give my soups depth and movement.

Hydrangea blossom

Hydrangea bead soup

Monochromatic Bead Soups

Color families can be defined in as narrow or wide a segment on the color wheel as you would like.

This hydrangea blossom (above) is considered "purple." In reality, it is comprised of blue-purple in the center of each floret, brightening to a red-purple on the edges. Some areas even move into a coppery color. When you look at the whole bloom, you will also see dark shadows and bright highlights that add to the complexity of the color.

Adding lots of colors in the purple family—from blue-purple to red-purple—is much more dynamic than sticking with a single hue. Equally important is the use of different saturations and values. Notice how the darker shades mimic shadows and lighter tints mimic the highlights.

Creating Monochromatic Bead Soup

When you make a bead soup, start with a single hue within the color family—even if you wish to expand to other colors later.

1

Choose palette

Choose a color palette that is pleasing to you. Here, I drew inspiration from the red clay soil and rocks (above) from my husband's family farm in Oregon. I then used the analogous template to define the color set. The rich, earthy colors of the inner ring of the color wheel closely match the variations in the red rocks.

Hint

The rich, earthy analogous colors lie on the inner ring of the color wheel from red-orange through red-violet. The complex, unsaturated tones have lots of black, but also a bit of the complementary color green. Echoing this green undertone in grey-green beads will mimic the depth seen in the pile of rocks.

2

Add single hues

Pour out piles of the main color in a variety of sizes, shapes and finishes (shiny and matte). Don't forget to include shadows (dark beads in the same color family) and highlights (brighter beads in the same color family).

3

Expand color family

Expand the color family by leaning to either side of the main color family. Use all the shapes and sizes from step 2 and include shadows and highlights.

4

Evaluate bead piles

Stand back and look at the colors. Using the bead scoop, scoop up and remove the piles that you don't love and add more of your favorites. Also scoop up any colors you want less of.

Bead Soup Recipe:
Red Clay

My husband's family farm in the Willamette Valley, Oregon, is blessed with rich, dark soil, perfect for the multitude of crops they have cultivated for generations. However, up in the hills, farmers have to contend with clay. The soil and rocks are pretty, and if you look closely, you will see all shades of red and brown. I created this bead soup mix the year my father-in-law passed away, and my husband spent months on end on the farm helping his brother work the farm and his family cope with the loss of a wonderful man.

5

Mix beads

Add more of your favorite beads. When you've obtained the desired mix of beads, use the bead scoop to mix them together.

6

Check soup for depth of color

Once the soup is thoroughly mixed, check to see if it contains the depth and movement you were looking for. Does it have texture, highlights and shadows, all sizes of beads? This soup lies within the inner rings of the saturated color wheel, so the shadows are a deep dark brown, and highlights are found in the shiny copper beads and the bits of gray "sand."

7

Add gems

Gems, pearls and shells within the same color palette add texture, depth and bright accents to the mix.

Blending Multicolor Bead Soup

When you are confident creating monochromatic bead soups then you are ready to create multicolor bead soups using the same techniques and the color wheel.

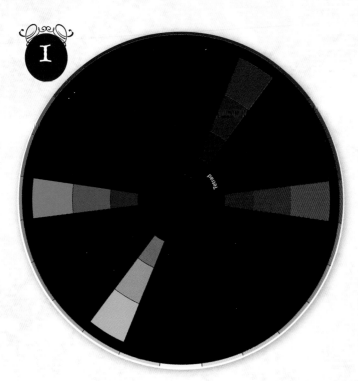

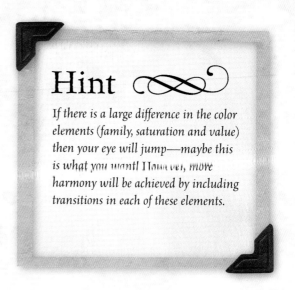

Hint

If there is a large difference in the color elements (family, saturation and value) then your eye will jump—maybe this is what you want! However, more harmony will be achieved by including transitions in each of these elements.

Choose color palette

I chose the cool, watery colors of teal (blue-green) and chartreuse (yellow-green) in the unsaturated, browned tones shown in the inner ring of the color wheel. This pair could be used on its own or in a number of other relationships including a tetrad with berry (red-violet) and coral (orange-red).

Make individual soups

Make monochromatic soups for each of the desired color families (see Creating Monochromatic Bead Soup on pages 20–21). Note that there are shadows and highlights in each soup, and that I have adjusted the size of each pile to reflect the relative amount I want in the final mix. I also decided to focus on only three parts of the Tetrad: blue-green, yellow-green and red-violet.

Add shadows

I thought more depth was needed as well as a transition between the chartreuse and berry, so I added an earthy brown soup that is unsaturated and lies inside all rings of the color wheel.

4

Include highlights

Adding some clear soup provides highlights to the whole soup and gives it a watery feel.

5

Mix colors

Adjust the size of each pile until they are of a proportion that looks good and you feel the soup has shadows, highlights and transitions. Mix all the beads together to see the overall effect.

6

Add gems

Gems fill out the palette and add significant points of interest because of their large size. Notice how the bits of coral fill in the fourth part of the tetrad. The clear quartz mimic drops of water and enhances all the other colors.

Hint

Gems are a great way to add pizzazz and transitions to a bead soup. I add the gems after achieving the desired mix of color families and feel that there are good transitions. Adding a handful of gems also provides dark shadows and a few bright highlights, helping the soup come alive!

Beadweaving Basics

Bead soups and freeform beadweaving are fabulous partners. Now that you know how to create gorgeous bead soups, get ready to start using them in the vast array of projects in this book. All are based on netting and peyote stitches, covered in this section, that are relatively fast and easy to learn. Before you attempt freeform beadweaving, it is important to gather the right materials and tools and to learn the basic stitches as outlined in this section. Those stitches will usher you into two fun and colorful projects in the next chapter—*Rippled Netting Bracelet* (page 47) and *Make Waves Bracelet* (page 52)—that will help you hone your skills with basic stitches and prepare you to break the rules when you launch into freeform work in subsequent projects!

Basic Beadweaving Kit

Grab a basket or box, or dedicate a drawer to the basic tools you will need for all the projects in this book. Specific materials will be called out for individual projects, but you will always need the following tools in your basic beadweaving kit.

Thread

There are a variety of beadweaving threads on the market, and everyone has their favorite. I like working with Fireline because it is strong and doesn't fray—it is also easy to thread into a needle. However, it is stiff and some people find it awkward to use. It also comes in very limited colors. Other great choices are Nymo or Conso, which come in a multitude of colors and feel supple, more like sewing thread.

No matter which thread you use, I highly recommend doubling it—especially when working in the netting stitch. Netting is a very loose stitch and some beads will only get one pass of thread. This means the thread can easily break if your piece gets caught on something or is under stress (like a bracelet, or near a clasp area). A doubled strand gives double the strength and double the integrity. If you work with a doubled strand and with the smaller seed beads in a bead soup mix (14/0 or 15/0), you will need to use a thin thread. Thin Nymo and Conso will be designated as size B and thin Fireline as 4 lb.

Beading Needles

To pass through the smallest beads more than once, I recommend using a size 12 needle. I prefer flexible "beading needles," which enable me to get into tight places. For those that like a shorter needle, or don't like it when the needle starts bending, then you might prefer a "Sharp" needle.

Beeswax

Because netting is a loose stitch, it is helpful to augment the thread with something that will help hold tension. Beeswax is sticky, and when coated threads pass against each other, they will slide less easily. (Don't confuse beeswax with lubricants that help the thread slide more easily. Lubricants are used for stitches with a tortuous path that load the beads.) Coating the doubled thread with beeswax also helps it stick together and act more like a single strand.

Thread Spool

Definitely not necessary, but very useful. When I need to transport a project or am just setting it aside for later, I wind my thread around a spool. Handy, inexpensive little spools can be found at many wool shops or online.

Bead Mat

Many projects in this book are best worked when laying flat on a bead mat rather than in your hand. The best mats are those that keep loose beads on top without rolling or bouncing off the surface and are neutral in color so the color nuances in your piece will stand out. It is also important that your needle moves smoothly without getting caught in the fibers or piercing through the fabric. My favorite mat is a 12" × 18" (30cm × 46cm) piece I cut out of white blackout cloth. Any fabric store will carry bolts of it; by buying just 1' (30cm), you can make three inexpensive bead mats. I often use an extra bead mat for my bead soup.

Bead Tray

If I am traveling or if my soup is large, I use a tray instead of an extra bead mat. I cut a piece of the white blackout cloth to fit exactly into the tray to help keep the beads from bouncing and for ease of picking them up with my needle.

Full Color Spectrum Lamp

This is one of the very best purchases I ever made! Working with tiny beads can be stressful on anyone's eyes (especially mature ones) and you

Thread burner tool

can never have too much light. Do your eyes a favor: invest in a good portable lamp with full color spectrum.

Glasses

Throw vanity out the window. If you kind-of, sort-of need glasses, put them on and save yourself from the eye strain of close-up work! You may also want to use magnifiers—either mounted on a light or on your head. They are kind of goofy looking but very useful!

Scissors

Buy good quality scissors with very sharp tips so you can cut thread close to the beadwork. And make sure these scissors are dedicated to beadworking only—no paper cutting!

Thread Burner Tool

It is not necessary, but a thread burner tool is one of those accessories I can't live without. A thread burner cuts thread very close to the beadwork and prevents frayed ends. Online sources are listed in the back, but your local bead store may carry them.

Ruler

Any ruler will do, but flexible ones are very handy.

Bead Scoop

These come in various shapes and sizes and are indispensable when mixing and cleaning up beads.

Hint

It took me many months of pain and numerous trips to a physical therapist to learn how important posture is. When I am working on a project, I become obsessed and forget to take care of my body. Following these simple steps will help you enjoy every moment of creating, without having to suffer for it afterwards:

• Sit up straight, with your shoulders rolled back and down.

• Bend only at your neck (not at your back).

• Put a pillow behind the small of your back if your lower back needs support.

• Use lots and lots of light!

• Every 20-30 minutes (set a timer if necessary), take a break and do the following. This little routine will only take about 30 seconds and is so important:

• Focus your eyes on an object in the distance (to ease the strain of keeping your eyes focused on a set focal distance).

• Roll your neck back to ease tension.

• Roll your shoulders in circles; end with them back and down.

Tips and Techniques

After beadweaving for a while, you can learn some very helpful tips. Here are a few things I've picked up through the years. These are only guidelines, so if you find a better way, then go for it (and pass on the hint).

Length of Thread

The optimum length of thread is one where you don't have to pull more than one time per stitch, nor have to change thread too frequently. I have found that holding the spool against one shoulder and pulling off a length in the opposite hand to as far as you can reach will mimic the distance from your beadwork surface to your stitching reach. (Of course, for a double strand, you will need to do this twice before snipping off the thread.) Any longer than this will mean you need to pull more than once per stitch for a while, and that, believe it or not, will really slow you down.

The only time a longer strand makes sense is if you are stringing on a very long first row (no actual stitching here). In this case, follow the instructions for optimum length then add the first row length (times two for a double strand).

Threading the Needle

Because the needle is rigid and the thread is flexible, it is easier to place the needle onto the thread, rather than the thread into the needle.

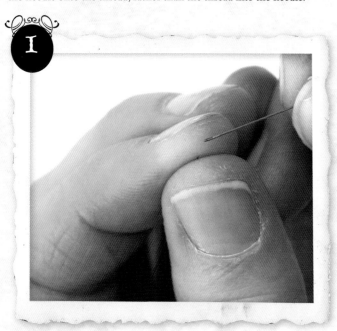

Thread needle

Pull the thread down through your thumb and index finger so the thread looks like a speck of pepper. Place the needle on top of the end of the thread. Push the eye of the needle onto the thread.

Waxing the Thread

Wax helps hold the thread together and maintain tension in your beadwork.

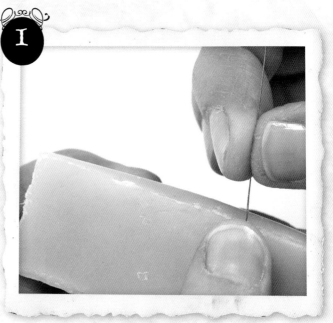

Wax thread

Hold the eye of the needle (to prevent it from chafing the thread) and draw the thread through the wax. Repeat a few times until the thread is coated well.

Adding a Stop Bead

Easily removable, a stop bead helps you string on the first row without losing a bead off the end of the thread.

Pick up bead

Pick up one bead in a different color from your intended beadwork. This will be the stop bead.

Thread bead

Pull the stop bead onto the thread, leaving a 4" (10cm) tail. Reinsert the needle into the bead, going in the same direction as before.

Make loop

Pull the thread tight. This will make a loop around the bead.

Later, when you want to remove the stop bead, just grab the bead between your fingers and gently pull it off.

Beginning and Ending Threads in a Project

It is always frustrating when you are working away and realize you are running out of thread and need to add some more. However, it is best to stop when you have at least 4" (10cm) to work with. When changing the thread, you rely on weaving the ends into the beadwork (as shown in the diagrams and the following steps) to secure the thread, not a knot! Knots become frayed, loosen with time and actually create a slight notch in the thread that can break if pulled. Only use knots to set the tension while securing the thread.

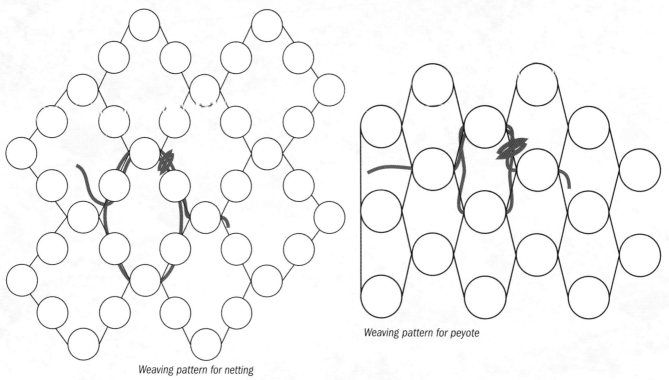

Weaving pattern for netting

Weaving pattern for peyote

Ending a Thread

This method allows you to better hide tails while reinforcing areas that would be weak if you only used a knot to finish the thread.

Secure Tension

To secure the tension within the beadwork, make a loop around the thread already in your piece at the location the thread is coming out of a bead.

Tie half-hitch knot

Pass the needle through the loop created from the last step to make a half-hitch knot around the thread in your piece.

Tighten knot

Pull to tighten the knot, making sure it cinches down around the thread in the location you looped rather than around a bead.

Weave away from knot

Pass the needle through beads to move away from where you just tied the knot.

Weave in a circle

To weave in a circle, you must change direction (see the diagrams on page 28). This can be done in front of a connector bead—just pass up through a bead on the other side.

Complete circle

Continue stitching through the beads in a circle, until you pass back through to where you tied the knot.

Once you go past the knot, use a pair of scissors or a thread burner to snip the thread as close as possible to the beadwork.

Beginning a Thread   Beginning a thread is very similar to ending one, just in reverse. The key difference is that you start the thread in a location away from where you ended the last thread because you don't want to overload the beads.

Start new thread

Pass through a couple of beads until you only have a small tail to hold on to.

Tie half-hitch knot

Pass under the thread to make a loop. Pass the needle through the loop.

Tighten knot

Cinch the thread to complete the half-hitch knot.

4

Stitch in circle

Thread through the beads in a circle, in the same manner as ending the thread (see step 5 on page 29).

5

Complete circle

Continue stitching through the beads in a circle, until you pass back through where you tied the knot. Using a pair of scissors, snip off the tail. Weave the working thread through the beadwork until you come to the spot where you left off.

Weaving in a Tail

Just as in starting and ending a thread, weaving in a circle will secure the tails from working loose with time.

1

Weave in circle

Thread a needle onto one end of the tail and weave it around in a circle as described in steps 4–6 on pages 29. Repeat for the remaining thread end.

Fixing a Broken Needle

Needles inevitably break, and with a doubled thread they can be stuck on the thread. Not to worry! There is a very easy way to change out the needle without losing any integrity in your piece or having to start a new thread.

Remove broken needle

Clip one side of the thread about 4" (10cm) away from the beadwork. Remove the needle and thread a new one onto the long end of thread.

Adjust thread

Adjust the length of the thread by moving the needle so the new tail is about 4" (10cm) long.

Stitch as normal

Hold onto both the old tail and new tail and continue to stitch into your beadwork as you would have done. You will be left with two tails that can be woven in later, and you will still have a doubled strand of thread in your beadwork.

Fixing a Knot

Knots happen. If you try to pull the knot apart with your fingers, you will always tighten it. So drop your thread and needle onto the mat and resist the temptation to touch with your fingers. My best advice is to stop, drop and pierce!

Stop, drop and pierce

Using two fresh needles (not the one in your piece, or you will risk tightening the knot as you work), pierce through the knot. It may take a while, especially if the knot is tight.

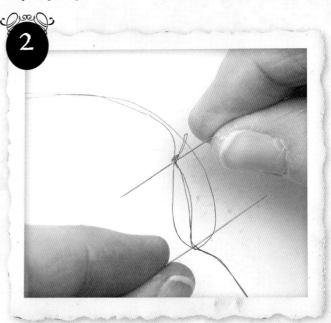

Pull apart with needles

Once you have pierced the knot with the two needles, gently coax the knot apart.

Backing Thread Out of a Project

Backing a double strand thread out of a project is easy, if you do it correctly.

Back needle out

When you are working with double strand thread and you need to backtrack, don't pierce the needle back through the bead you need to back out of, or you'll get a big knot. Pull the thread backwards until the needle reaches the bead opening. Gently back the eye-side of the needle through the bead opening.

Adding a Snap Closure

Sew-on snaps provide a secure, hidden closure option. I often choose them when the beadwork itself is busy or so full of movement that I don't want it visually broken up by a visible clasp.

The best snaps to use are found in fabric stores. I typically use size 1, 2 or 3 depending on the project and often use a pair of snaps for large, heavy necklaces.

Sew on one side of snap

Start a new thread (see Beginning a Thread on page 29). Weave it to the location you would like to add the snap. Weave in and out of the snap holes then through the beads in the piece. Each hole must be reinforced three times with the double strand of thread before moving on to the next snap hole.

Line up snaps

Line up the snaps properly before sewing on the second snap. Repeat step 1 to secure the remaining snap half.

Button Closures

Buttons and loops provide a decorative closure for bracelets and necklaces. Any button will work, with or without a shank.

Attaching a Button With a Shank Many buttons have a loop on the backside called a shank—these buttons are very easy to attach.

Place button

There should be at least ½" (1cm) of beadwork to allow space for a button closure. Start a new thread away from the button location and weave up to where you want to attach the button. Coming out of a bead on your piece, add a bead or two, stitch through the shank of the button and add another bead or two on the other side.

Secure button

Stitch into your beadwork to secure the button in place. Pull to eliminate any exposed thread. Weave around your beadwork until you are able to reinforce this loop of beads with the shank at least two more times.

End thread

Once the button is secure, end the thread by making a loop around the thread in your piece.

Make knot

Pace the needle through the loop to create a half-hitch knot, and pull to tighten. Then weave around in a full circle (see Ending a Thread on pages 28–29).

Adding a Button Without a Shank If your button does not have a shank, then you can make one as shown here.

①

②

Place button

There should be at least ½" (1cm) of beadwork to allow space for a button closure. Start a new thread away from the button location and weave up to where you want to attach the button. Coming out of a bead on your piece, add three or four 11/0 seed beads and stitch through one hole in the button. Make a loop of 11/0 seed beads that fill the space between the holes on the button. Pierce back down through the other hole and add the same number of 11/0 seed beads on the underside of the button before stitching into the beadwork.

Loop on underside of beadwork

Thread on three or four beads and piece back up into the button hole, going through some of the beads you already added.

③

Secure button

Reinforce the beaded shank and loop of beads on the back at least two more times by stitching around in the circle they make. Then tie a half-hitch knot around the thread in your piece, weave around in a full circle and clip your thread (see Ending a Thread on pages 28-29).

Hint ∽

Oftentimes the beadwork on your piece becomes overloaded with thread, and you run the risk of breaking beads if you stitch into them again. This is especially true if the beadwork is made with 14/0 or 15/0 seed beads as in the Rippled Netting project. In this case, you can just pierce through the beadwork, add a loop of 11/0 seed beads on the back and reinforce the button by stitching in a circle through the loop of 11/0 seed beads.

Adding a Loop Closure   Buttons require a loop on the other side of the piece to complete the closure.

1

Add loop

Add a new thread (see Beginning a Thread on page 29) and weave your way to the edge. Add a string of beads long enough to fit around the button. Weave through a bead on the other edge and pull.

2

Check fit

Check the fit of the loop around the button. If the loop is too small, you can pull the thread out and add more beads. If it fits, then you will need to secure the loop.

3

Position needle

Weave around the beadwork so the needle comes back out at the base of the loop.

4

Secure loop

Stitch through the loop at least two more times. Follow the instructions for Ending a Thread (page 28) to complete the closure.

Making Jump Rings

You may purchase jump rings, but they can be costly and are not necessarily in the size you want for your project. However, with the right tools and some wire, they are very easy to make. Choose the gauge of wire based on the size you want for your jump rings. The size you can make your jump rings depends on the diameters available on your round-nose pliers. For heavier projects, I use a medium to heavy gauge wire, such as 16-gauge, and use the widest part of the pliers. Check out the basic wireworking kit on page 111 to learn about the tools you will use.

1

Place wire in pliers

Cut a length of wire at least 3" (8cm) long. Using round-nose pliers, grasp the wire at the location on the pliers corresponding to the diameter you want for your jump rings.

2

Turn wire onto pliers

Turn the pliers to form a circle, allowing the tip of the spiral to move away from the base.

3

Make coil

Keep coiling the wire until you have used up all of the wire and the coil is moving down the length of the pliers.

4

Clip end

Using your flush-cut wire cutter with the flat side facing into the coil, clip off the straight end.

Cut first jump ring

Turn your wire cutter so that the flush cut is facing the opposite direction—toward the end you just cut. Slide the cutters until they rest against the tip of the wire and are positioned to cut into the second ring. Cut to make first jump ring.

Check jump ring appearance

The piece that falls off should look like an open ring with flat ends on both sides.

Cut more jump rings

What's left on the coil will have a pointed edge. Turn the flat side of the flush-cut wire cutters into the coil and trim off the pointed edge. Be sure to put your thumb over the pointed end as you cut to keep the little, pointed piece from flying away.

Repeat to use up coil

Continue rotating the pliers in the manner described in step 7 to get flat edges on all the rings.

Close jump rings

Press the ends of the jump ring together in a scissor fashion to close the circle.

Work harden jump rings

With a flat bench block or anvil, strengthen the jump ring by work hardening with the smooth end of a chasing hammer.

Adding Earwires

Make smaller beadweaving projects into earrings by adding earwires.

Open loop

Using the chain-nose pliers, open and close the loop in a scissor fashion so you don't change the shape of the loop.

Add earwire to piece

Pierce the earwire through the loop on your piece.

Close loop

Using the chain-nose pliers, close the loop in the scissor fashion

Beadweaving Stitches

All of the projects in this book are based on two very fast and easy-to-learn stitches: Basic 3-Bead Netting and Basic Even-Count Peyote. Instructions for both basic stitches follow, and once you master them, you will be ready to dive into the freeform beadweaving projects in the next chapter.

Basic 3-Bead Netting

Netting is a fast and easy stitch. It can be worked either horizontally (as seen in the diagram below, the first row defines the width, then additional rows build up the length) or vertically (the first row defines the length and subsequent rows build up the width). I have also included a diagram to help you visualize the stitching pattern. Throughout this stitch and all others in the book, maintain good tension with the thread and beads—pull tight to eliminate any exposed thread in between the beads.

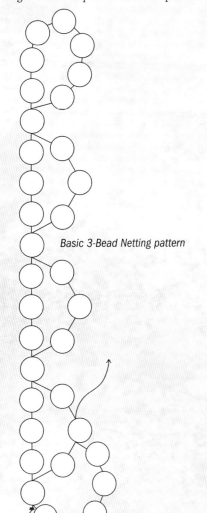

Basic 3-Bead Netting pattern

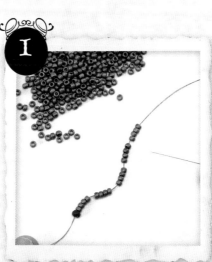

String first row

With a double strand of waxed thread in a comfortable length (see Length of Thread on page 26), put on a stop bead (see Adding a Stop Bead on page 27). String beads in sets of four for the desired width of your piece.

Turn corner

Count back from your last bead and pass back through the eighth bead from the end. Pull to form a loop on the end.

Begin pattern

Pick up three beads and pass into the fourth bead to make a scallop of three beads on either side of a shared bead. (This is shown in the diagram on page 39.)

Continue pattern

Continue to pick up groups of three beads, passing into the fourth, until you reach the end of the row. The final bead you pass into should be the very first one strung onto the first row and will lie next to the stop bead.

Remove stop bead

The working thread and tail should now be coming out of the same first bead. Remove the stop bead by pulling on it.

Secure tension

Pull on both the working thread and tail to eliminate any exposed thread and to ensure that the scallops lie evenly distributed on either side of the shared beads. Tie a half-hitch knot to maintain the tension. Do *not* cut the tail.

7

Turn corner

To turn the corner, pick up five beads and pass into the center of the last group of three beads from the previous row. Pull tight. (Don't worry about the asymmetrical lobe laying off the end—it seems out of place now, but will tie into the pattern once you get going.)

8

Build up row

Add a group of three beads and stitch into the center of the scallop in front of you—again, this is the fourth bead from where your thread is exiting.

9

Stitch to top

Keep adding groups of three beads and passing into the center of the scallop ahead until you reach the top scallop. The top center bead can be a little tricky to see—remember to count four beads from the current location of your thread.

10

Continue pattern

Turn the corner as in step 7. Notice that the asymmetrical lobe below is balanced out by the one you just added. Continue building up the pattern by repeating steps 7-9 until your piece is the desired length. Refer to pages 28-30 for directions on ending thread, starting a new one and weaving in the tails.

Basic Even-Count Peyote

Peyote is a versatile stitch and is the basis for many projects in this book, as well as three-dimensional work. Peyote is a tighter stitch than netting, so it works a little slower but has a very supple, fabric-like texture. Once you get past the first few rows, it becomes easier.

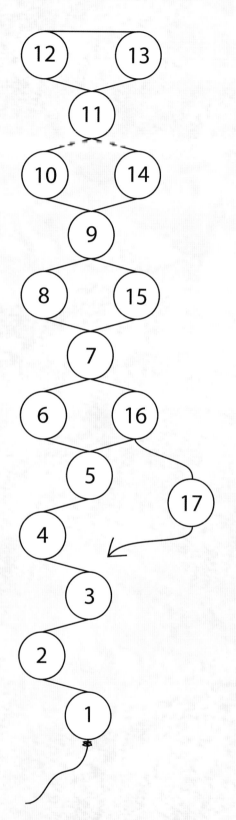

Even-Count Peyote pattern

1

Begin stringing

With a double strand of waxed thread in a comfortable length (see Length of Thread on page 26) put on a stop bead (see Adding a Stop Bead on page 27). String beads to the desired width of your piece, making sure there are an even number. (Here, I have strung on twelve beads.)

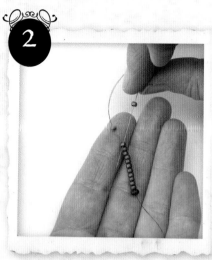

2

Turn corner

Pick up one bead. Skip over one bead and pass into the second one from the end (not including the bead you just picked up). In the diagram, you will pass into bead #11.

3

Position bead

Pull the thread to tighten it, and with your finger, force the two end beads to lay side-by-side on either side of the one you stitched into. (See beads 12 and 13 in the diagram.)

4

Build up row

Pick up one bead, pass across one bead, then stitch into the next bead (bead 9 on the diagram). Pull the thread to maintain tension.

Pattern emerges

Keep picking up one bead, skipping across one and stitching into the next bead. You will see a pattern emerging—the row you first strung beads onto is now being split into the first and second rows of peyote. The beads you are now adding are technically the third row.

Remove stop bead

At the end of the row, pull off the stop bead and adjust the tension to eliminate any exposed thread and to force the beads to lie in the pattern shown. Tie a half-hitch knot between the working thread and tail to maintain tension. Do not cut your tail.

Turn corner

To turn the corner on this row and all others, pick up one bead, skip over the last one you came out of and pass into the second bead.

Build up rows

Continue to pick up one bead, skip over one and pass into the next to build up this and all other rows. Note that you are really just filling in a little space from the last row with your new beads.

Refer to pages 28–30 for directions on ending thread, starting a new one and weaving in your tails.

Journey Into Color & Freeform Projects

Freeform beadweaving is a journey. An opportunity to travel in different directions each time you pick up your bead soups! As with all freeform art, you may start with an idea, but the materials—and your mood—may pull you off in completely unexpected and beautiful directions. For this reason, no two of my pieces are ever the same! This is exciting, stimulating and spawns all kinds of new ideas— something I hope to instill in you as we venture forward. I realize though that it can be a bit overwhelming when you're taking your first steps, so I invite you to journey along this new and creative path with me.

We will start with Projects with Basic Stitches section (page 46) so you can hone your skills using netting and peyote stitches and get you comfortable pushing the boundaries. Once you have the basic stitches down, it is time to throw out the rules and launch into pure Freeform Beadweaving (page 56). You will wander down many paths with your bead soups, incorporating gorgeous materials along the way: large accent beads, fibers and ultimately beach glass and shells in Beadweaving with Beach Finds (page 72).

The Wanderlust Beadweaving section (page 82) is for those who love adventure! By mixing structure into the freeform stitches, we will create swirls and caves and dips and curves—like a gorgeous landscape full of texture and unexpected turns. Next, color comes alive in Freeform Color Flow (page 98) where you will learn how to move seamlessly from one color to the next to create palettes that literally glow. And for the ultimate mix of materials in Beadweaving on Metal (page 110), you will blend textures, colors and mediums. Here you'll combine metal that is hammered and shaped with delicate beadwork to make gorgeous wearable art.

As we wander together, I will share my inspirations for each project and color palette. I hope that by walking along with me you will feel increasingly confident forging your own freeform paths, you will find colors around you that make you happy, and you will discover inspirations of your own to make your freeform pieces truly from your heart.

So grab your color wheel, basic beadweaving kit and some bead soups, and let's see where this journey will take us!

Projects with Basic Stitches

Try these fast and fun projects to hone your skills with the basic stitches before throwing away the rules and launching into freeform beadweaving in the rest of the book.

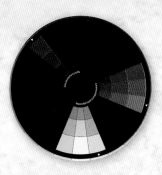

RIPPLED NETTING BRACELET

Explore movement, color and texture in this bracelet made in Basic 3-Bead Netting. The ripples offer a great opportunity to start using your color wheel to enhance your palette.

The bracelet is made up of a background of smaller seed beads with ripples of increasingly larger beads at periodic intervals. The background color is dominant in quantity and surrounds all of the ripples, so choose this color first. When choosing seed beads and gems for the ripples, you have so many design options: repeat one color scheme or make each ripple different; blend the ripples with the background or introduce new colors. As you become more advanced in blending bead soups, try the color flow technique in the Freeform Color Flow section (page 104).

BEAD SOUP RECIPE:
Autumn Leaves

Autumn is cozy sweaters, walking home from school with leaves crunching underfoot and fires in the fireplace. I love the cool, crisp, misty mornings, warm afternoons and the deep, rich colors of autumn—a dramatic split complementary.

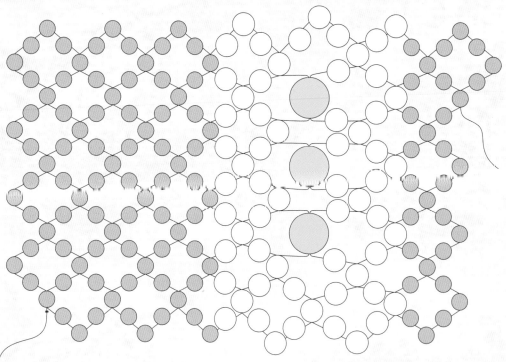

Rippled Netting pattern

Netting is an asymmetrical stitch, so a few tricks are needed to fool the eye if you want to achieve pseudo-symmetry. Note on the diagram that each time you transition from one bead size to the next, two of the previous beads are carried into the first stitch. You will start each ripple and increase the size of beads on rows going up, and you will end each ripple and decrease the size of beads on rows going down.

1

Create base

Stitch at least five rows of Basic 3-Bead Netting with the 14/0 or 15/0 background beads (see Basic 3-Bead Netting on page 39). Make sure to hold the piece in your nonworking hand and work toward your working hand without flipping the piece.

2

Turn corner to start ripple

Start every ripple at the bottom of your piece and work toward the top. Add two background 14/0 seed beads then three 11/0 beads in the color you chose for the first ripple.

Begin ripple

These five beads allow you to turn the corner into the first ripple. Now pick up three 11/0 beads for the next scallop. Refer to the diagram to visualize the pattern.

Build up ripple

Build up the ripple with two full rows (one up and one down) of the 11/0 beads, then turn the corner with five 11/0 beads.

Begin center row

The center row of the ripple consists of three stitches made by picking up a single gem and passing into the center of the next scallop. Note that the gem placement is asymmetrical because of the seed beads you added at the bottom to turn the corner.

Complete center row

Once you have three scallops made of a single gem each, turn the corner with five 11/0 beads and pass into the top gem.

Hint

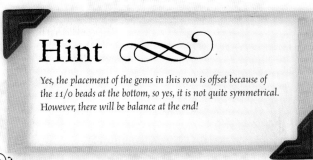

Yes, the placement of the gems in this row is offset because of the 11/0 beads at the bottom, so yes, it is not quite symmetrical. However, there will be balance at the end!

Start decreasing ripple

Start decreasing on a downward row with two full rows of the 11/0 beads: one row down stitching into the gems and one row back up to the top.

Complete the ripple

Add two 11/0 beads and three 14/0 background beads to turn the corner back into the background beads. Hold tight to maintain tension as shown in the hint below.

Hint ∽

The most difficult part of this project is maintaining adequate tension to force the ripple to pop up and out of the plane of the background and to avoid exposed thread—especially when decreasing bead size. To do this, you need to curve the piece around your finger and don't let go! Let the phone ring, don't answer the door and cross your legs if you have to!

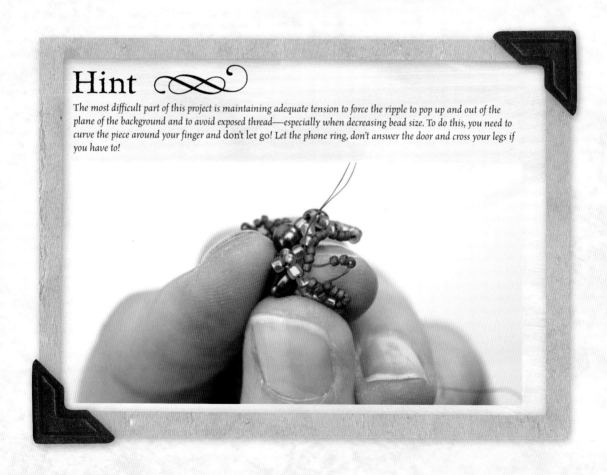

Let go when secure

Once you have obtained good tension (sometimes it takes a couple of tries), it won't be secure until you have stitched at least two or three rows of the background. Now you can let go. Continue to work in Basic 3-Bead Netting until the next ripple.

Complete bracelet

Repeat steps 2–9 until you have built up the bracelet to the desired length. Both ends of the bracelet should have at least ½" (1cm) of background to allow space for a closure.

Attach the closure (see Adding a Snap Closure, page 32, and Button Closures, on page 33, for more information).

Hint 〰

I avoid counting rows whenever possible so I just eyeball the number of background rows between ripples. As long as I keep the piece in the same orientation and always begin an increase when going up and begin a decrease when going down, then it is easy to see when I need to start a new ripple. Usually this works out to be 5 rows.

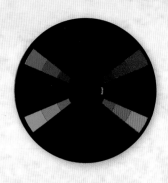

MATERIALS

basic beadweaving kit

13 grams of 11/0 seed beads for the background

bead soup in colors that complement the background

small (3mm to 5mm) accent beads in colors that complement the bead soup

snap for closure

MAKE WAVES BRACELET

Peyote with a splash! Play with color and bead soups to really make waves. Use this technique for a bracelet or choker and dramatically change the look by incorporating one huge wave or a series of ripples. The background area of the piece will be made with a base color of 11/0 seed beads. The raised, multicolored waves are accents made using a bead soup.

To get in the mood, try listening to some old time surfing music. My favorite album in this genre is a Starbucks compilation *Big Waves*. If this doesn't take you to Highway 1 along the California coastline, then you owe yourself a vacation!

BEAD SOUP RECIPE:
The Carnival

When I was little, I loved the vibrant combination of red, orange and blue—the colors of balloons, wrapping paper, carnivals and always my choice of pegs for Mastermind, a game my brother Carl and I would play. Carl was eleven years older than I, so our childhoods belonged to different eras—his well rooted in the 1960s; mine a decade later. As diverse as we were in age and personalities, we both loved games of strategy like Othello, chess and Mastermind, and would play for hours. I think I was really pretty good, or perhaps Carl made concessions for a little girl. Yes, my Mastermind pegs were always red, orange and blue. Did he ever notice?

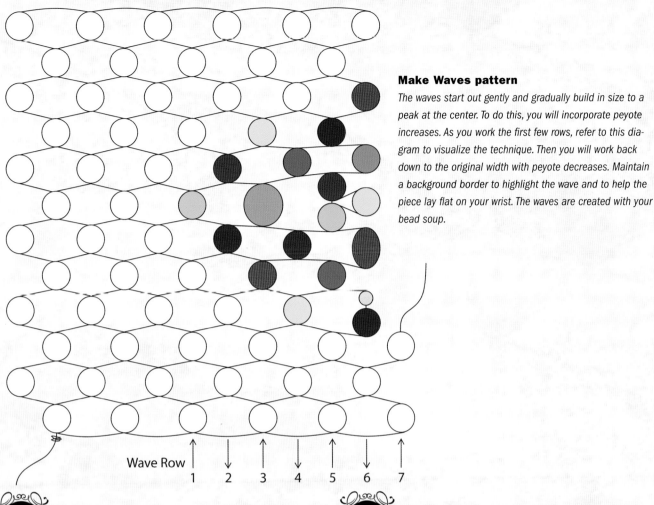

Make Waves pattern

The waves start out gently and gradually build in size to a peak at the center. To do this, you will incorporate peyote increases. As you work the first few rows, refer to this diagram to visualize the technique. Then you will work back down to the original width with peyote decreases. Maintain a background border to highlight the wave and to help the piece lay flat on your wrist. The waves are created with your bead soup.

Wave Row   1   2   3   4   5   6   7

Create base

With twelve beads as your starting row, build up at least ½" (1cm) of Basic Even-Count Peyote (see page 42). This will give you something to hold onto, and leaves options open when you go to decide whether you want one large wave or a series of smaller ripples.

To start the wave, work the first three stitches using the background color.

Begin wave

Now pick up one bead from your bead soup in the same size as the background (11/0), but in a different color. Go back to the background color and complete the row. The colored bead will lay just off center along the width of the piece.

Add second row of wave

Work the first two stitches using the background bead color. Work the next two stitches with 11/0 beads from your bead soup so that there are now three colored beads in your wave. Go back to the background bead and complete the row.

Add third row of wave

Work the first two stitches using the background bead. Work the next three stitches with beads from the bead soup. You can start to increase by introducing a larger size bead near the center. Go back to the background bead for the last two stitches.

Set width of wave

Continue to introduce beads from your bead soup in the middle of the wave until only three columns of background color are on the top and bottom of the wave.

Increase wave

From here on, work the first two and last two stitches in the background bead. Increase in the middle for the next few rows by incorporating larger beads or two beads in the space of one near the center.

By making the length of beads you are adding just slightly greater than the hole you are placing them into, your wave will bulge out gently. When you add more than one bead per stitch, you will have more stitches on future rows. This is peyote increase and is shown above and on rows 4 and 6 of the diagram on page 53.

Hint

Keep tension so there is no exposed thread.

7

Decrease wave

Continue adding beads from your bead soup to the center area of each row until you have achieved half of the wave length you desire.

In the center, start decreasing by choosing slightly smaller beads from the hole you are placing it into. As always, work the first two and last two stitches using your background color.

8

Hint ∽

You may have to decrease faster than you think to achieve a uniform wave.

Decrease number of beads

Stitch one bead in place of two when you can. (Your goal is to work down to the same number of beads that you started with, until you're back to twelve columns.)

9

End wave

As you work down to the right number of stitches and all 11/0 beads, gradually decrease your use of the bead soup so the border becomes larger and there is just one colored 11/0 bead in the near center.

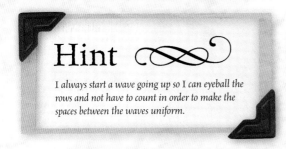

Hint ∽

I always start a wave going up so I can eyeball the rows and not have to count in order to make the spaces between the waves uniform.

10

Create space between waves

If you want to incorporate more than one wave, you must pre-plan to determine how many waves you want and how far apart you would like them. In this sample, the waves are about ½" (1cm) long and the space between them is about ¼" (6mm) or about 7 rows, which appears as three beads between the last wave and the next.

Work you pattern until you have built up the bracelet to the desired length. Both ends of the bracelet should have at least ½" (1cm) of background to allow space for a closure.

Attach the closure (see Adding a Snap Closure, page 32, for more information).

Freeform Beadweaving

Now that you are comfortable with the basic stitches it is time to throw away the rules and embrace unpredictability! The following projects introduce freeform beadweaving and give you the skills to tackle more challenging projects.

Freeform beadweaving draws on your right brain—the creative flow of color and texture without order. In pure freeform work there is no form, all preconceived ideas are thrown out the window and the piece itself starts telling you where it should go. As you read through this book, you will see that most of the projects are a combination of structured stitches and freeform. I often begin with an idea of what I want to make and incorporate some boundaries, such as forcing the ends of a necklace to come together at the back of the neck, yet allow the center portion to go wild.

Bead soups and freeform beadweaving are perfect partners. The kinks and bends that occur with variations in bead size become fabulous opportunities for texture. The diversity of color and surface finishes gives the finished piece depth and movement.

Freeform Earrings (page 57) lays out the fundamentals of freeform netting. Once you have mastered the general concepts, the paths you can take are limitless—Wandering Path Necklace (page 61) and Wander with Flare Necklace (page 64) are pure freeform and quite easy and fast. Rocks and Rolls Bracelet (page 67) combines freeform netting with basic netting worked in circular form. It all leads into the next section and down one of my favorite paths—to the beach. So grab some bead soup and come wander with me!

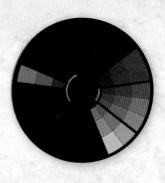

MATERIALS

basic beadweaving kit

10–20 grams seed bead soup plus handful of small (3mm–5mm) accent gems and beads

2 fairly identical accent beads for top of earring

pair of earwires

FREEFORM EARRINGS

Throw off all constraints! These elegant earrings are a fast and easy project made with freeform vertical netting. Freeform netting sounds like a liberating technique—and it is! I use the words "about" and "approximately" in these instructions because your turns and weaves will depend on the beads you string on. Follow these instructions, and give or take a bead (or a few) here and there, to create a pair of earrings for every outfit in your closet!

BEAD SOUP RECIPE:
Dark Chocolate

OK, I admit it—I am a chocoholic. Especially dark chocolate, with a few nuts and perhaps with an exotic spice or two. Did you know that dark chocolate is good for you?! And for organic, fair trade (read: guilt-free) chocolate, I love Theo Chocolate—a Seattle chocolate treasure. If you ever visit Seattle, make a tour of Theo's top on your list!

These browns come from the earthy inner circle of the color wheel and go still deeper into the center. Notice that even in this darker palette there are darker shadows, bright highlights and also a variety of colors from gold-brown to purple-brown. Some beads even have blue undertones.

2

String on random mix of beads

With a double strand of waxed thread in a comfortable length (see Length of Thread on page 26), put on a stop bead (see Adding a Stop Bead on page 27), leaving a 4" (10cm) tail. String on a mix of beads from your bead soup, avoiding gems and special accent beads. (This row establishes the length of the earring that will hang below the large accent bead.)

Turn corner

Lay the strand on the mat with the tail away from you (it will become the top of the pendant).

Turn the corner at the bottom of the earring by passing back through about the eighth bead from the end or any prominent bead that will allow your loop to lie nicely. (In this case, it works better for me to go through two beads. Consider these beads as the shared bead for rows 1 and 2 just as you would have in Basic 3-Bead Netting.) Adjust the tension to remove gaps.

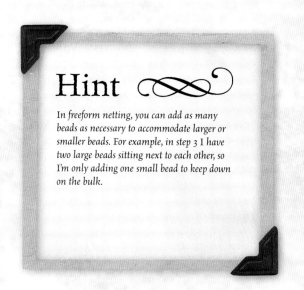

3

Hint

In freeform netting, you can add as many beads as necessary to accommodate larger or smaller beads. For example, in step 3 I have two large beads sitting next to each other, so I'm only adding one small bead to keep down on the bulk.

Build up second row

Add a few beads and pass back through a bead from the first row that lies next to the strand. When you pass through this bead, your piece should neither lean dramatically toward the first row nor the second. If it does, adjust the number or size of beads in the strand you just added or pass through a different bead from the first row.

4

Stitch to top

Continue to work up the strand until you reach the top and pass back through the first bead from row 1. Remove the stop bead (adjust the tension to remove any gaps) and make a knot between the working thread and the tail.

5

Add accent bead

String on the accent gem. Next add ten 11/0 seed beads. Pass back through the gem to form a loop of seed beads on top. Now you are ready to build up the earring.

6

Stitch down

As you add more beads, pull the thread to tighten the beaded loop. Work down the earring with random strands of beads.

7

Turn corner without adding beads

When you reach a bead near the bottom, pass the thread through the beads on the bottom loop and come out a bead on the other side.

Hint

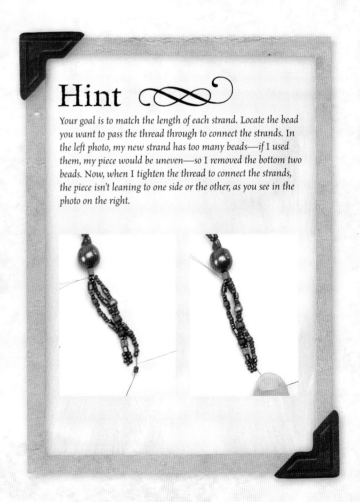

Your goal is to match the length of each strand. Locate the bead you want to pass the thread through to connect the strands. In the left photo, my new strand has too many beads—if I used them, my piece would be uneven—so I removed the bottom two beads. Now, when I tighten the thread to connect the strands, the piece isn't leaning to one side or the other, as you see in the photo on the right.

Stitch to top

String on random lengths of beads, stitching into the piece where each beaded section ends.

Build up earring

When you reach the top, pass through the accent gem and loop of beads on top to reinforce this area at least twice.

Continue building up the earring and adding accent gems until you are pleased with the overall shape, texture and color balance. End the thread and weave in the tails (see Beginning and Ending Threads in a Project on page 28).

Repeat for other earring

Follow steps 1-9 to make a second earring to complement the first. The second earring doesn't have to be identical.

Add earwires to the small loop above the focal bead (see Adding Earwires on page 38).

Hint

The easiest way to make identical earrings is to make both at the same time (stitch by stitch), in mirror image. But consider letting loose to make an asymmetrical pair!

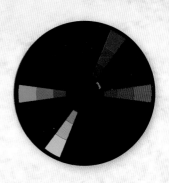

MATERIALS

basic beadweaving kit

50-80 grams seed bead soup plus a handful of accent gems and beads

snap or other clasp

WANDERING PATH NECKLACE

Making this necklace is like strolling in the garden: you're free to take any path you chose with a plethora of colors to enhance your bouquet. Come walk down the path with me, but feel free to veer off and forge your own trail—there is no right or wrong way.

BEAD SOUP RECIPE:

Tropical Surf

The bead soup (created in Blending Multicolored Bead Soup on page 22) has a peaceful, watery feel like the rich colors of a tropical surf. Reminiscent of blue-green water, bits of coral and bright green tropical fish, this soup makes me want to grab my snorkel and head out to the reef.

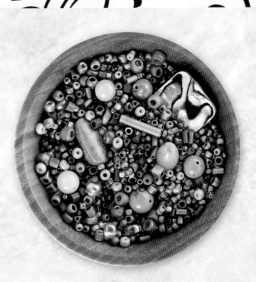

String first row

Determine the length of your necklace and add ½" (1cm) to allow for a closure.

   With a double strand of waxed thread in a comfortable length (see Length of Thread on page 26) that's a little longer than normal to allow for the first row, put on a stop bead (see Adding a Stop Bead on page 27), leaving a 4" (10cm) tail. String on a random assortment of beads from your bead soup to the determined length.

Work ends in Modified 3-Bead Netting

Turn the corner by passing through approximately the eighth bead from the end. Employ Modified 3-Bead Netting (see page 63) for the first 5" (13cm) to reinforce the back of the necklace.

Begin freeform beadweaving

Now it is time to follow your own path. String on a random length of beads and pass into a bead from the first row. Continue in this manner, altering the length of the beads you add to provide textural interest until you reach the last 5" (13cm) of the necklace.

   For the last 5" (13cm) employ Modified 3-Bead Netting until the end of the row.

   Remove the stop bead. Tie a knot between the working thread and the tail. Turn the corner with approximately five beads.

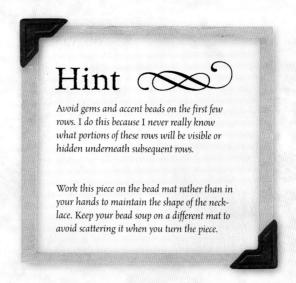

Hint ∞

Avoid gems and accent beads on the first few rows. I do this because I never really know what portions of these rows will be visible or hidden underneath subsequent rows.

Work this piece on the bead mat rather than in your hands to maintain the shape of the necklace. Keep your bead soup on a different mat to avoid scattering it when you turn the piece.

4

Build up necklace to desired width

Follow steps 2–3 to build up at least four rows of freeform beadweaving with 5" (13cm) of Modified 3-Bead Netting on each end.

By the fifth row, or once you know which side of the necklace will face out, start adding accent gems, pearls and special beads. As you build up the necklace, feel free to pass over and under strands from previous rows.

When you are happy with the overall design, weave in all loose threads (see Weaving in a Tail on page 30). Attach a closure of your choice (see pages 32–35).

Hint

As you add accents, keep in mind these color questions: Do you have dark spaces that act as shadows or negative space? Are there bright bits of highlights popping through? Do the colors blend together for a peaceful look or contrast with each other for a more stimulating look? Keep building up your piece until you are satisfied with its overall color, texture and thickness.

Modified 3-Bead Netting

Some areas of your piece will get a little more stress than others—where you open and close the clasp, on a necklace where you untangle your hair or clothes from the strands behind your neck, or on a bracelet where it rests on your computer keyboard or hits the table. In these areas of high stress, I minimize long, loose strands of beads and use Modified 3-Bead Netting. This is a variation of Basic 3-Bead Netting and is worked as follows:

Pick up approximately three beads and pass into approximately the fourth bead as in Basic 3-Bead Netting. The difference is that the actual number of beads you add is not important. Rather, the goal is to match the length of beads you add with the length of the beads you pass over. You can check this with your piece laying flat on the mat. Pull the thread very tight to eliminate any exposed thread. If your piece stays flat and straight—great! If it bends, then the length of beads you are adding is different from the length you are passing over. Adjust as necessary.

Length of added beads don't match

If it bends, the length of beads you are adding is different from the length you are passing over. Adjust as necessary.

Length of added beads match

If your piece stays flat and straight, you are correctly stitching using the Modified 3-Bead Netting method.

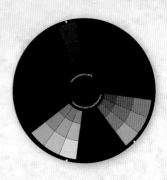

MATERIALS

basic beadweaving kit

50-80 grams seed bead soup plus a handful of accent gems and beads

mix of fibers including yarn, ribbons, thread—your imagination is the limit

scissors

snap or other clasp

WANDER WITH FLAIR NECKLACE

This is an exciting variation of the *Wandering Path Necklace*. By adding fibers to the beadwork, you open up a whole new world of color and texture!

The harmonious combination of beads and fibers adds a rich complexity to the color and texture of your piece, just as a mix of grapes lends depth, complexity and a rich aroma to Spanish and Portuguese red table wines. Surrounded by bead soup, yarns and ribbons, a glass of wine, and Portuguese fados on your sound system, you will be ready to wander down a path bursting with color and flair.

BEAD SOUP RECIPE:
Olive Branch

Every evening when Dad came home from work, we would sit in the living room by the fire, listen to classical music, talk, read and have wine (or juice) and hors d'oeuvres—perhaps a tin of almonds or a bowl of marinated olives—sometimes more if we had guests. Mom still does this every evening when we come to visit. In doing so, she continues to nurture the warmth of spending time together at the end of every day and has passed on the gracious tradition of hors d'oeuvres to my sons.

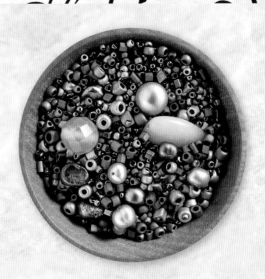

Choose fibers

Choose fibers in the same way that you chose the accent gems in the bead soup. They may blend with the soup or complement the colors. Make sure you have shadows, highlights and a variety of textures.

Begin wander technique

Follow steps 1-3 of the Wandering Path Necklace (page 61), completing two full rows of stitches. Leave some open loops in the freeform section.

When you complete 5" (13cm) of the Modified 3-Bead Netting section in row 3, start introducing fibers. Sew through the first fiber and pass back into the beadwork to secure it.

Hide thread

You may need to flank the fiber with beads to hide the thread. When needed, add a strand of bead soup to help position the fiber where you want it.

Weave fiber into beadwork

Using your fingers, weave the fiber in and out of the open loops in the freeform section, allowing for extra-long tails. When you reach the end, do not secure the fibers or cut the tails.

Add fibers

Add fibers, one by one, in the same manner until you have achieved the complexity of texture and color you desire (you can always add more later).

Secure fibers and fill in necklace

Weave strands of beads in freeform style, occasionally passing the needle through fibers to secure them. Weave into each fiber in at least five or six spots to secure it to the necklace.

Introduce gems and other special beads in amongst the fibers for added depth and texture.

When you reach the end of the freeform section, build up the ends with 5" (13cm) of Modified 3-Bead Netting.

Remove fiber tails

Build up the center with additional rows of beads and gems until the fibers are secure and the necklace is filled out to your satisfaction.

When the fibers are secure, use the scissors to trim off the ends.

Complete the necklace

If desired, hide the ends of the fibers using more passes with beads on the top of the piece.

Weave in all loose threads (see Weaving in a Tail on page 30). Attach a closure (see pages 32–35).

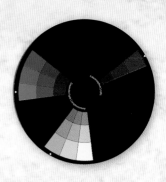

MATERIALS

basic beadweaving kit

30 grams seed bead soup plus a handful of small accent beads

14 grams 11/0 seed beads

mandrel (I use a size 10 round paintbrush handle)

closure

ROCKS AND ROLLS BRACELET

Like old time rock 'n' roll, this bracelet is a diverse mix of styles. The rocks are formed with freeform masses of bead soup kept in line by rolls of uniform tubular netting. Beatles, The Mamas & The Papas, Creedence Clearwater Revival, Journey, Pink Floyd—put on some ole rock 'n' roll, sing at the top of your lungs, and pump out a few of these bracelets!

BEAD SOUP RECIPE:

Rain Forest

I would love to tell you I was on a trip to the tropical rain forest and took pictures of lush green vines dripping with vibrant flowers and exotic birds—but I wasn't and didn't. This palette was created the other way around. I pulled out my color wheel, found a combination that intrigued me and played around with it, first using collaged bits of paper torn from old magazines. An image and theme started to appear—I soon realized that I wanted to use three parts of the tetrad, skipping the purple, and as I worked, it brought to mind lush green vines dripping with vibrant flowers and exotic birds.

67

PROJECT NOTE: Calculating the Length of the Bracelet

This bracelet is formed with two types of sections. The rolls are tubular netting sections ⁷⁄₁₆" (12mm) long, or about six rows. The rocks are freeform areas that start out about 1½" (4cm) long and reduce down to about 1" (2.5cm). To calculate the number and size of these sections, measure your wrist (including how loose you want the bracelet), subtract ½" (1cm) and divide by 1½" (4cm). This is the total number of roll-and-rock segments you will need, plus one more roll for the other end.

1

Begin first row

With a double strand of waxed thread in a comfortable length (see Length of Thread on page 26) put on a stop bead (see Adding a Stop Bead on page 27), leaving a 4" (10cm) tail. String sixteen 11/0 single-color seed beads. Pass back through the first bead to make a circle.

2

Begin pattern

Place circle onto the mandrel. Add three beads. Pass over three and stitch into the fourth bead.

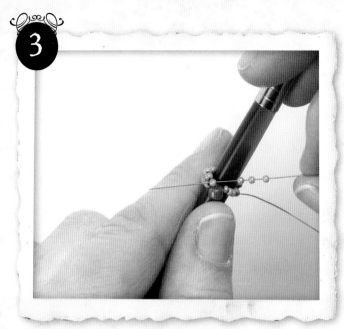

Complete second row

Continue the pattern described in step 2 around the circle until you pass back through the first bead of the first row.

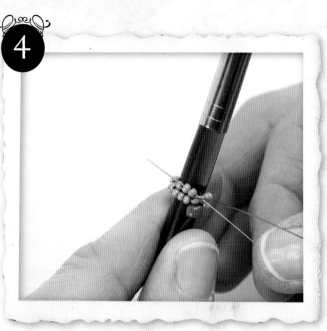

Step up into new row

Now you need to "step up" into the next row by passing through 2 beads from the first scallop added in the previous row. This will place your needle in the middle of a scallop and position it to add the next row.

Build up roll

To start the third row, add three beads and pass through the center of the next scallop, just as you would in Basic 3-Bead Netting.

Hint

Every time you start a new row, you will step up two beads. The new row will start in the middle of a scallop.

Hint

As you finish a row, it's sometimes hard to see what bead to go into before stepping up. Make sure to go into the first bead from the last row. You can determine it by counting four beads from where your thread exits.

Complete first roll

Continue in this manner, building up the roll to a total of 6 rows (or about 7⁄16" [12mm]); make sure you step up in the same way for each row and finish the roll by stepping up.

Separate the rolls by a 1½" (4cm) strand of beads from your bead soup.

Begin second roll

Start the next roll by adding sixteen 11/0 single-color seed beads and pass back through the first of these to form a loop at the top of the bead soup strand. Place it onto the mandrel. Follow steps 2–6 to build up the roll.

Complete rolls

Repeat steps 2–7 until you have a number of rolls separated by strands of bead soup and the total length (when rolls are squared to the ruler) is what you calculated at the beginning. **Note:** The rocks will reduce in size as you work, so this should be too big for your wrist.

Fill in rock sections

Fill in the rock sections with freeform netting by adding a few beads from your bead soup and passing into a bead from the initial row. Continue until you reach the next roll, then pass into a few beads and change direction to work your way back to the initial roll.

Complete rocks

Stitch back and forth between all the rolls to build up the rocks. Add gems and other accent beads as you fill in around the entire circle until you are happy with the result. Make sure you only reduce the length of each rock by ½" (1cm) so the bracelet will fit comfortably around your wrist.

Weave in all loose threads (see Weaving in a Tail on page 30). Attach a closure (see pages 32–35).

Beadweaving With Beach Finds

I grew up overlooking Puget Sound with Mount Rainier as a backdrop, in a little fishing town inhabited by old Scandinavian and Polish families. At the base of a 300-foot cliff below our house lays our beach—a little difficult to get to, but well worth the hike. It's not a sandy beach, nor one with ocean breakers, but full of other treasures. On the neighboring beach still stands a little dilapidated shack only accessible by water—the destination of any teenager with a boat.

I remember my Dad cursing the "wild partiers" who would throw their bottles onto the beach. But the lapping waves did their part and turned those sharp shards into treasures. Anyone who ventured down to the beach would cram multicolored rocks, broken shells and beach glass into every available pocket, pouch and bag then hiked up the steep, winding road to our house quite a few pounds heavier. Over the years, I have accumulated piles of beach treasures. And for decades they were buried in bowls, boxes and drawers, each awaiting a time to be rediscovered and given new life.

The following projects will build on the freeform beadweaving techniques you learned in the previous section to encapsulate these finds and turn them into spectacular treasures—no holes needed! *Beachcomber Pendant* (page 73) uses freeform peyote to make a single pendant. Freeform netting is used in *Wander Down the Beach Necklace* (page 77) to connect numerous pieces of beach glass and shells. A gallery section follows, featuring wearable objects of art with a mix of stitches to give you even more ideas for your own treasures.

So head out to the beach with a big bag, backpack or deep pockets, and comb the beach with an end purpose in mind!

MATERIALS

basic beadweaving kit

beach glass or other found object from the beach (I recommend starting with a triangular shape)

30 grams seed bead soup plus a handful of small accent gems and beads in colors to complement found object

leather, chain, fibers or strung beads to hang pendant from

BEACHCOMBER PENDANT

Bags bulge with treasures after a day at the beach. Transform these shells, beach glass, stones and other finds into extraordinary pendants with freeform peyote techniques that will inspire you to comb the beaches!

BEAD SOUP RECIPE:

Coral Beach

My Aunt Carolyn "had her colors done" in the 1980s when Color Me Beautiful was all the rage (I still carry around my copy). The cool undertones of the summer palette set off her delicate creamy skin, grey-brown eyes and light brown (now silver-grey) hair. However, she also looks fabulous in some of the peachy colors of spring. Her color consultant left her with fabric swatches in every color family and labeled her expansive palette "Summer Twilight."

Note that the red-orange is unsaturated and lies on the inner ring of the pastel wheel in contrast with the other two colors from inside the saturated wheel. Coral Beach is a blend from her palette that consists of three parts of a tetrad.

Circle around beach glass

With a double strand of waxed thread in a comfortable length (see Length of Thread on page 26), put on a stop bead (see Adding a Stop Bead on page 27), leaving a 4" (10cm) tail. String on a random mix of your bead soup, avoiding gems and long bugles, until it is long enough to wrap around the beach glass. Adjust the number of beads until it fits snug without gaps and complete the circle by passing through the first bead (don't stitch through the stop bead; it will be removed in the next row).

Build with peyote stitch

Remove the beach glass. You will now work the Basic Even-Count Peyote stitch (see pages 42–43). Choose beads that fit nicely into the spaces they are placed in without making bends or buckles in the circle. Pick up one bead, pass over one bead and stitch into the next bead. Continue in this fashion to build up row 3 of peyote (remember that the bead strand you started with splits into rows 1 and 2 and the row you are now adding is technically row 3).

Place beadwork on beach glass

After completing row 3 (by passing into the last bead from the initial strand), place the peyote circle around the beach glass to ensure it fits. Leave the beach glass on the piece. Remove the stop bead and tie a knot between the tail and the working strand.

Step up into row 4 by passing through the first bead of row 3. From now on, hold the strand in place on the beach glass.

Build rows and incorporate freeform stitches

Build up row 4 by working on the beach glass and keeping the tension high to avoid exposed thread. For all rows from this point on, you can deviate from the Basic Even-Count Peyote stitch by:

· Adding more than one bead and jumping over stitches to make holes.
· Adding large seed beads to make bends.
· Passing through beads from the previous row, without adding beads, to make an indentation.
· Adding large gems for accents.

5

Secure beach glass

Come out of the peyote band somewhere in the middle of the beach glass. To find an attractive location, place the thread in a line around the beach glass, and string a length of bead soup around the beach glass until it is long enough to stitch directly into the peyote circle on the backside.

Add or subtract beads and adjust the tension until the new strand fits snug against the beach glass without gaps. Stitch into a bead on the back to help set the ending location.

6

Build up cross-strand

Peyote stitch around to the front (or change direction by weaving through the piece) to reinforce the cross strand. Subsequent passes will strengthen it both structurally and visually.

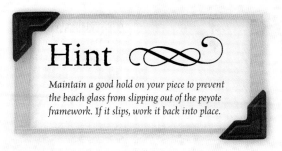

Hint

Maintain a good hold on your piece to prevent the beach glass from slipping out of the peyote framework. If it slips, work it back into place.

7

Add webs between strands

When you add cross-strands, the joints can look stilted—as if they are there just to secure the beach glass (they are—but you don't want them to look like it). To achieve a more organic look and soften the angles, make a web of peyote stitches between the strands as shown. You can begin adding accent gems and beads.

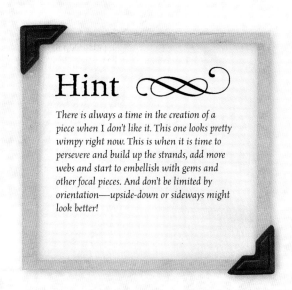

Hint

There is always a time in the creation of a piece when I don't like it. This one looks pretty wimpy right now. This is when it is time to persevere and build up the strands, add more webs and start to embellish with gems and other focal pieces. And don't be limited by orientation—upside-down or sideways might look better!

Secure beach glass

Keep adding strands and building them up until the beach glass is secure and you are pleased with how it looks.

Add bale

To add a bale, start a new thread coming out of the top of the piece (see Beginning and Ending a Threads in a project on page 28). String on a strand of beads long enough to make a loop that will pass over whatever you'll hang it from. You can build up that strand with peyote or freeform netting or just by reinforcing the strand.

When you are satisfied with the strength of the bale, weave in all remaining tails (see Weaving in a tail on page 30). Sting the pendant onto a desired length of chain of your choosing.

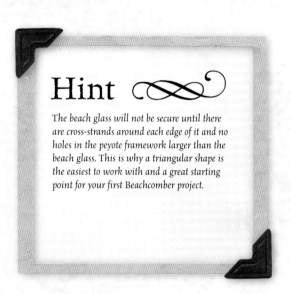

Hint ∽

The beach glass will not be secure until there are cross-strands around each edge of it and no holes in the peyote framework larger than the beach glass. This is why a triangular shape is the easiest to work with and a great starting point for your first Beachcomber project.

Hint ∽

Instead of a bale, you can add a pin or incorporate your piece into a larger work of art.

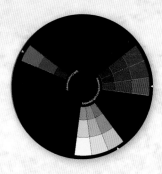

MATERIALS

basic beadweaving kit

focal pieces of stones, shells, beach glass or any other found object that is of a size and shape conducive to the final design

30-60 grams seed bead soup plus a handful of small accent gems and beads in colors to complement the found objects

WANDER DOWN
THE BEACH NECKLACE

Encase and interconnect shells, beach glass, stones and other pieces to create flowing, organic works of art. A perfect end to a day on the beach!

Don't worry if you can't make up your mind when you begin designing the piece. Because this project is freeform and organic, it can evolve, change shape and grow as you work. Many of my projects end up very different from the original design. The only thing you really need to determine is whether you are happy with how the bead soup looks with the beach treasures. If you are happy with it, then you are ready to start beading!

BEAD SOUP RECIPE:
Sandy Beach

We are all drawn to memories of our childhood—mine being in Puget Sound. My husband feels at home in pastoral farmland. Both can be found on Whidbey Island, Washington—a long thin slip of land tucked into the middle of Puget Sound with commanding views of the Cascades to the east, Olympic Mountains to the west.

Sandy Beach captures the essence of our Whidbey Island beach where flat rocks, oysters, moon snails, driftwood and Dungeness crab abound, and the sand is an amalgamation of brown basalt, white granite, bits of shells and unsaturated accents from the inner ring of the color wheel.

Lay out design

Design your piece by laying out your beach finds on the bead mat. Arrange the focal pieces into a pleasing pattern and pour the bead soup around them. Manipulate the soup with your fingers until you like the design. If you have a camera, take a picture, or sketch out the basic shape.

Begin long first strand

If you are going to make a very long piece, it is easiest to work in smaller segments that incorporate three to four focal pieces at a time and connect them later.

    With a double strand of waxed thread in a comfortable length (see Length of Thread on page 26) put on a stop bead (see Adding a Stop Bead on page 27), leaving a 4" (10cm) tail. String on a random mix of your bead soup until you have reached the length you defined for your piece, plus a generous amount to allow for curves and bends around the focal pieces. I usually add 25 percent to 50 percent in length.

Build up beadwork frame

Turn the corner and work your way back to the beginning of the strand with freeform netting stitches in varying lengths (see *Wandering Path Necklace* on pages 61–63). Remove the stop bead and tie a knot between your tail and working threads.

    Turn the corner again and work your way up the beadwork with freeform stitches. This time, you may want to incorporate holes that could wrap around some of the focal pieces.

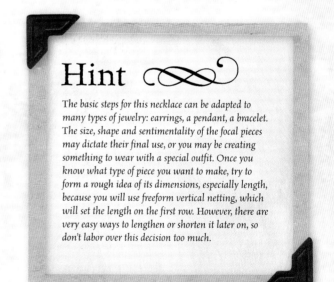

Hint

The basic steps for this necklace can be adapted to many types of jewelry: earrings, a pendant, a bracelet. The size, shape and sentimentality of the focal pieces may dictate their final use, or you may be creating something to wear with a special outfit. Once you know what type of piece you want to make, try to form a rough idea of its dimensions, especially length, because you will use freeform vertical netting, which will set the length on the first row. However, there are very easy ways to lengthen or shorten it later on, so don't labor over this decision too much.

Place first focal piece

Once you have built up your beadwork with a few rows of freeform netting, it is time to incorporate the focal pieces and secure them one by one. To do this, set a focal piece in place and maneuver the beadwork frame so it spreads around the focal piece as much as possible. When you get the focal piece in place, hold it with your non-working hand.

Build netting around focal piece

Weave the thread through the beads until you are coming out of a bead as close to the bottom edge of the focal piece as possible. String a random mix of beads on the back of the piece and, while maintaining good tension, stitch into the framework on top of your piece.

Build up this strand in the same way you did for the *Beachcomber Pendant* using freeform netting instead of freeform peyote.

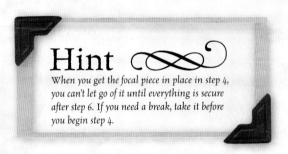

Hint 〰

When you get the focal piece in place in step 4, you can't let go of it until everything is secure after step 6. If you need a break, take it before you begin step 4.

Secure focal piece

Referring to the directions for *Beachcomber Pendant* (see pages 57–58, steps 5–8), add cross-strands and webs to secure the focal piece. Remember that the piece will not be secure until there are cross-strands around each edge and no holes in the netting framework larger than the focal piece. Keep adding strands and building them up until the focal piece is secure and you are pleased with how it looks.

Repeat steps 4–6 to add the remaining focal pieces one at a time and build up the framework around each piece.

Weave in all loose threads (see Weaving in a Tail on page 30). Attach a closure (see pages 32–35). (For earrings or pendants, add a bale onto the top of the beadwork.)

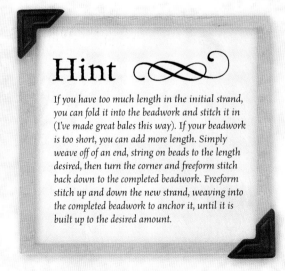

Hint 〰

If you have too much length in the initial strand, you can fold it into the beadwork and stitch it in (I've made great bales this way). If your beadwork is too short, you can add more length. Simply weave off of an end, string on beads to the length desired, then turn the corner and freeform stitch back down to the completed beadwork. Freeform stitch up and down the new strand, weaving into the completed beadwork to anchor it, until it is built up to the desired amount.

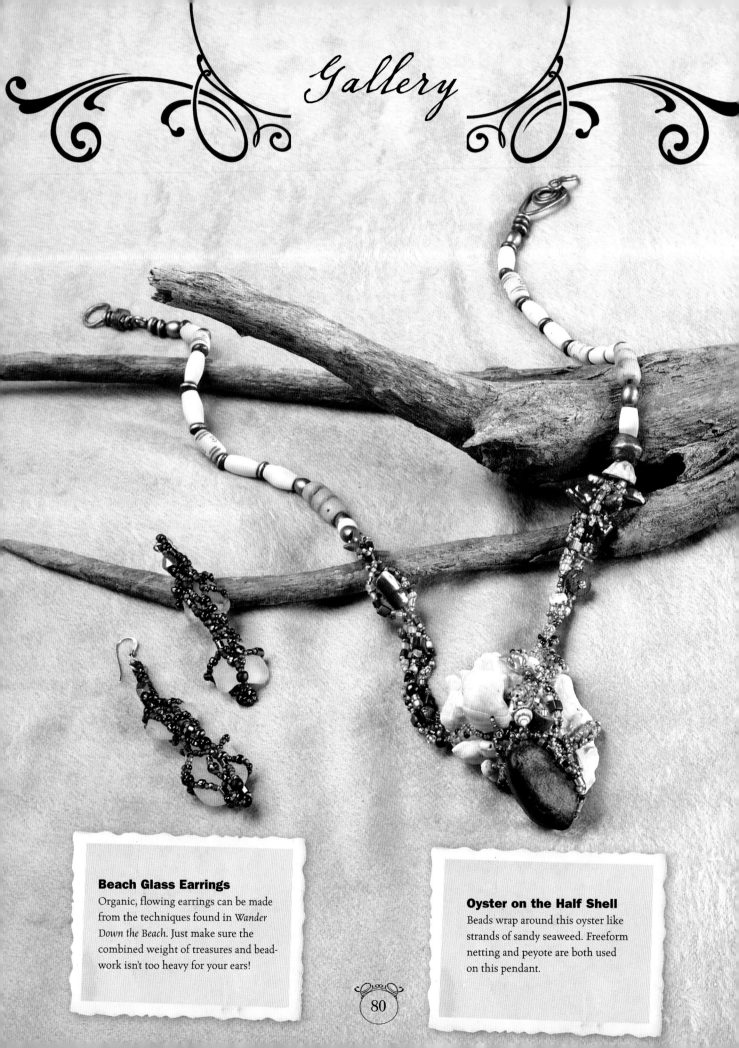

Gallery

Beach Glass Earrings

Organic, flowing earrings can be made from the techniques found in *Wander Down the Beach*. Just make sure the combined weight of treasures and bead-work isn't too heavy for your ears!

Oyster on the Half Shell

Beads wrap around this oyster like strands of sandy seaweed. Freeform netting and peyote are both used on this pendant.

Grandma's Beach Lariat

Wander Down the Beach techniques
can be expanded into a full necklace, like this lariat made from
beach glass gathered from my
Grandma's beach on Vancouver
Island. An intact bottle top provides the perfect connection.

Wanderlust Beadweaving

Come wander with a purpose! The Wanderlust series introduces some control and new stitching techniques to the pure freeform of the previous sections with dramatic results—expect lots of compliments when you wear them (and be prepared to go shopping for the perfect outfit to go with them).

Play with color, texture and form to create elegant, wearable art using both controlled and pure freeform vertical netting. You will learn how to make beautiful curves and waves that add depth and intrigue to your piece and provide spaces for focal points such as bezels, stones and other treasures. The Wanderlust techniques will experiment with freeform style and bead soups, and encourage you to break the rules, but always with an end design in mind!

Wanderlust Bauble Earrings (page 83) are an excellent place to start because they are fast and easy and teach you the basics of Wild Modified 3-Bead Netting (page 84), which is used in all of the Wanderlust projects.

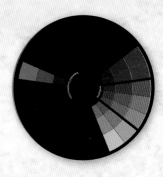

MATERIALS

basic beadweaving kit

30 grams seed bead soup
plus small accent gems
and beads

2 fairly identical accent
beads for inside of earring

pair of earwires

WANDERLUST BAUBLE EARRINGS

Make colorful earrings, pendants or components with these sassy baubles. They are a quick and easy introduction into working with the bends created by forcing larger beads to line up against smaller ones in Wild Modified 3-Bead Netting.

BEAD SOUP RECIPE:

Copper Penny

Copper is my favorite metal whether it is old, new, tarnished or shiny. Among my collection of old pots in varying sizes and conditions is a relatively new one: a huge copper soup pot. Years of use on my gas stove with soups dripping over the sides have lent an irresistible patina to the pot. I have dreams of faux painting my kitchen to match!

Begin earrings

With a double strand of waxed thread in a comfortable length (see Length of Thread on page 26) put on a stop bead (see Adding a Stop Bead on page 27), leaving a 4" (10cm) tail. String on a mix of beads from your bead soup, avoiding gems and special accent beads. Keep stringing until the strand is 4" (10cm).

Turn the corner by passing back through about the eighth bead from the end—or any prominent bead that will allow the loop to lie nicely. This bead is a shared bead for rows 1 and 2 just as you would have in Basic 3-Bead Netting (see page 39). Adjust the tension to remove gaps.

Stitch second row

Stitch the entire length in Wild Modified 3-Bead Netting (see below for the technique).

End second row

Continue to work up the strand with Wild Modified 3-Bead Netting until you reach the top and pass back through the first bead from row 1. Remove the stop bead. Adjust the tension to remove any gaps and make a knot between the working thread and the tail.

Wild Modified 3-Bead Netting

Wild Modified 3-Bead Netting is a variation of the Modified 3-bead Netting on page 63. In this case, you want your piece to bend with each stitch.

Add about three beads. Skip over approximately three beads from the first row and pass through the next bead. The number of beads you add and skip over is not important. The key in this case is to purposely mismatch the length of the strand of beads you add and the beads you pass over. In this way, the piece will start to bend, which is what you want.

You can check this with your piece laying flat on the mat. Pull the thread very tight to eliminate any exposed thread. If the piece bends slightly—great! If not, then the length of beads you are adding is too similar to the length you are passing over. Adjust as necessary.

Build up wild area

Turn the corner with approximately five beads and stitch into a prominent bead in the first scallop. Continue stitching with Wild Modified 3-Bead Netting for a total of at least three rows to accentuate the bending in the netted beadwork.

Twist beadwork

On the fourth row, twist the bead work so it lies in three dimensions. (I usually try to create a circle on a vertical plain intersected with one on a horizontal plain.) Secure the bauble by stitching between beads and adding beads if necessary.

Add focal bead

Add a focal bead in the middle if desired. Work the thread to a position just above the hole in the focal bead. You can either weave it through the existing beads or add beads.

Add loop

Once you have secured a pleasing shape, add a beaded loop on the top. Weave in all loose threads (see Weaving in a Tail on page 30). Add earwires (see Adding Earwires on page 38).

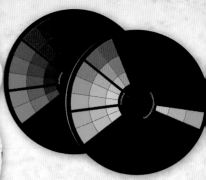

MATERIALS

basic beadweaving kit

60-90 grams seed bead soup plus small and medium accent gems and beads

large focal bead for center of bracelet (optional)

size 3 snap

WANDERLUST BRACELET

The *Wanderlust Bracelet* celebrates the large bends and bulges that result as larger beads are forced to line up against smaller ones. In the first few rows of vertical netting, these bends are exaggerated. Then we will force the bracelet to lay straight by 'crunching' it. When this happens, the ends of the bracelet will be structured so that the piece fits nicely around your wrist but the middle will go wild!

BEAD SOUP RECIPE:
Blue Ice

When I was growing up, we used to hike in the Cascade Mountains just a few hours from home. On the slopes of Mount Rainier were ice caves that we could climb into and marvel at the full spectrum of blue and green light filtering through the ice. Unfortunately, the remaining ice caves have melted so much that they aren't safe to hike into. This Blue Ice Bead Soup is in memory of those beautiful mountain gems.

PROJECT NOTES
Review stitch pattern

Recall that the ends in Wandering Path Necklace were Modified 3-Bead Netting (see page 63) and that the Wanderlust Baubles were entirely comprised of Wild Modified 3-Bead Netting (see page 84). In this bracelet, we will use Modified 3-Bead Netting for the ends (2" [5cm] on either side) and Wild Modified 3-Bead Netting for the entire middle section. Once the bracelet shape is secured, we will move into pure freeform netting (see pages 58–69).

Determine how long to make the beadwork

The bracelet is comprised of approximately 11 to 13 rows of vertical netting—the first row defines the length. To determine what length you should start with:

1. Measure snug around your wrist.
2. Add ½" (1cm) to allow for snap closure.
3. Add 2½"–3" (6cm–8cm) or more, depending on how tight you would like your bracelet and how much crunch you want (the more crunching, the more length you need to start with).

Create tame ends and wild center

With a double strand of waxed thread in a comfortable length (see Length of Thread on page 26), a little longer than normal to allow for the first row, put on a stop bead (see Adding a Stop Bead on page 27), leaving a 4" (10cm) tail. String on a random assortment of beads from your bead soup, avoiding gems and special accent beads, to the length determined above.

Turn the corner by passing back through about the eighth bead from the end—or any prominent bead that will allow the loop to lie nicely. Adjust the tension to remove gaps and stitch in a tight Modified 3-Bead Netting for the first 2" (5cm).

After 2" (5cm), stitch in Wild 3-Bead Netting for the center portion of the bracelet. Keep the tension tight to eliminate any exposed thread.

Stitch the last 2" (5cm) in Modified 3-Bead Netting to the end. Remove the stop bead and turn the corner. Continue to build up your beadwork with 2" (5cm) of Modified 3-Bead Netting at each end, using Wild Modified 3-Bead Netting in the middle.

Let piece curl on mat

As you build up rows, keeping the ends flat on the mat and accentuating the bends in the middle, your piece will start to curl around itself.

Hint

Is your piece bending severely in one direction? Great! Accentuate it! If it bends away from the row you're adding, let it go further by adding larger and more beads. If it bends towards the newest row, put on less and smaller beads to keep it bending. You can also make holes by putting on more beads and skipping one or more scallops from the previous row.

3

Hint

Don't feel constrained by how your piece is behaving when you crunch it. If you can't find a pleasing shape, try flipping the ends over on themselves, or folding them into the center and creating new ends. Remember, this is freeform!

Crunch the center

When you have added about half your desired width (about 5–7 rows), it is time to crunch the piece and add a center focal bead if you wish.

Force the bracelet to lie in a straight line on the mat—the center will stick up from the mat in swirls and caves. Arrange these swirls into a pleasing shape, with the ultimate goal of keeping the ends straight and in line with each other.

4

Secure shape and add gems

When you are happy with the shape, you can secure it. Stitch shorter strings of beads over or under the previous rows and across the caves to hold the bracelet in place.

The caves and swirls in the beadwork are perfect for filling with large focal beads. Stitch these into place while you secure the shape. If you have added a very large, heavy bead, you may need to reinforce it with more than one pass of thread.

5

Build up width

Build up the width until the ends of the piece are straight, in line and of uniform thickness. The center can be the same thickness or larger, depending on what is pleasing to you and what your bracelet wants to do.

Weave in all loose threads (see Weaving in a Tail on page 30). Attach the snap closure (see Adding a Snap Closure on page 32).

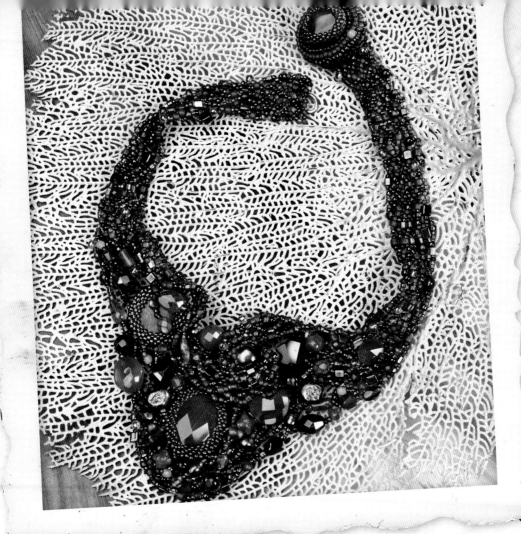

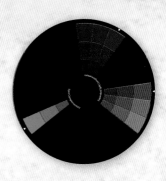

MATERIALS

basic beadweaving kit

120-150 grams seed bead soup plus small and medium and large accent gems and beads

large focal beads, gems, treasures or bezels for center of neckpiece

WANDERLUST NECKPIECE

Take the *Wanderlust Bracelet* to a new level with this dramatic neckpiece! The techniques are similar, but with longer dimensions and different sculpting. A bezel closure provides an elegant touch, but feel free to add a simpler closure to keep the focus up front. Be prepared for oooh's and aaaah's whenever you wear this neckpiece.

BEAD SOUP RECIPE:

Nebula

In the 1970s, my Dad worked in Los Angeles Monday through Friday, but we lived in Gig Harbor, Washington. Sometimes we would join him for a week or so, and he would take a couple of days off to vacation with us.

We would each get a day to choose the activity, and on one of these occasions, my Dad chose to take us to the Mount Palomar Observatory. I was entranced with the beautiful pictures of the stars, planets and nebula that lined the observatory walls—this was in the days before Hubble made these pictures widespread.

My Nebula bead soup is in memory of that trip, which made such an impact on me and showed me all of the beautiful colors of the universe.

PROJECT NOTE: Determine Necklace Length

The base strand is comprised of approximately 11 to 13 rows of vertical netting—the first row defines the length of your strand and the overall size of your neckpiece. This strand needs to be long enough to allow for a flat band around your neck and a lot of waves, crunches and curls in the center. To determine what length you should start with:

1. Length of Ends (L_E): Measure from collarbone to collarbone around the back of your neck. Subtract ½" (1cm) to allow for the bezel clasp and divide the resulting figure in half—this is the length of the Modified 3-bead Netting section on each end of the strand.

2. Length of Middle (L_M): The middle section needs to span across your chest in the arc you would like. For instance, if you want your neckpiece to lay across your collar bone in a gentle 'U', then that distance may be 4"–5" (10cm–13cm), or if you want the piece to lay lower on your chest, the distance may be 10" (25cm). Now you must allow for curling, crunching and waves, and the amount you add is dependant on how much crunching you envision. I typically take my proposed arc length and generously double it—then I let my piece show me where it wants to go, and even if it is not what I planned, I've never been disappointed.

3. Total Length (L_T): The total length of your base strand is the length of both ends plus the midsection: $2L_E + L_M = L_T$

String first row

With a double strand of waxed thread in a comfortable length (see Length of Thread on page 26), significantly longer than normal to allow for the very long first row, put on a stop bead (see Adding a Stop Bead on page 27), leaving a 4" (10cm) tail. String on a random assortment of beads from your bead soup, avoiding gems and special accent beads, to the length L_T determined above.

Turn the corner and build up the neckpiece base strand by following instructions for the *Wanderlust Bracelet* (see page 86) but with the lengths you determined above.

Build up base and shape into neckpiece

Both ends should be worked in Modified 3-Bead Netting for the length L_E determined above.

The entire middle section should be worked in Wild Modified 3-Bead Netting and you should avoid gems, pearls and other accent beads. Continue to build up the neckpiece base strand to at least five rows.

Lay the base strand on the bead mat and force it into a 'U' shape. The ends will lay parallel to each other and should still be the length L_E you calculated earlier. The center area will fold and curl into a knot of beadwork.

Place accent gems

Manipulate the shape of the neckpiece by placing the large gems and accent beads into some of the swirls and caves created in the base strand.

4

Secure gems

When you are happy with the shape, secure it with strands of beads and gems as described in *Wanderlust Bracelet* (see steps 4–5 on page 88). Continue to build up the neckpiece until the ends are a width that looks good to you and the center portion seems balanced.

Add the larger gems and beads as desired.

Add shadows and highlights

Include a variety of color values from deep dark shadows to bright highlights by stitching on additional beads. (Here, the tiny pieces of bright orange really make the pallet pop.)

When you are finished, weave in all loose threads (see Weaving in a Tail on page 28) and add a closure. I used a bezel closure (see page 92) to finish this piece, but you can use the closure options detailed on pages 32–35 if you prefer.

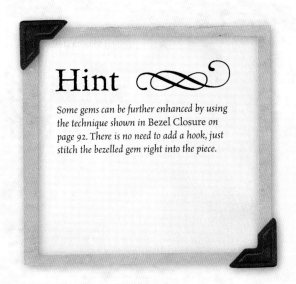

Hint

Some gems can be further enhanced by using the technique shown in Bezel Closure on page 92. There is no need to add a hook, just stitch the bezelled gem right into the piece.

MATERIALS

flat-bottomed bead, stone, button etc.

2 pieces of ultra-suede

glue appropriate for both fabric and glass or stone (I use Ultimate)

5 grams each of seed beads in 11/0 and 14/0 or 15/0 sizes

assorted seed beads for bead embroidery

metal jump ring at least 8mm–10mm in diameter

4" (10cm) 18-gauge wire in color that works with your bead soup

flush-cut wire cutters

round-nose pliers

chain-nose pliers

chasing hammer

anvil and pad

scissors

BEZEL CLOSURE (OPTIONAL)

By this time, many hours have gone into your neckpiece, and your closure should provide a beautiful finishing touch that enhances the overall design. Instructions for a *Bezel Closure* follow, but your design might cry out for a hidden snap or a stunning button. You need to design your closure to fit your neckpiece and your style. The *Bezel Closure* will give you another technique at your disposal, even if only to be used for coordinating earrings!

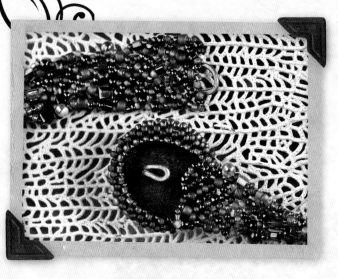

Hint

When choosing the focal object for the bezel, your choice should take into account color, shape, texture and size. You could use a dramatic button in a bright accent color then bezel it with neutral colors from your palette to anchor it into the design. Or maybe the stone is neutral and the seed beads add the spice. Perhaps a small gem off to one side of the bezel is all the drama your piece needs. The options are endless!

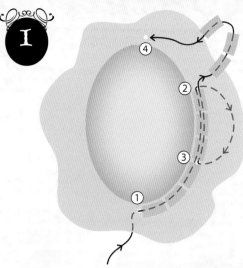

Prepare stone for bezelling and stitch first row of bead embroidery

Glue the flat stone, button or bead to the ultra-suede leaving a boundary of ultra-suede at least ½" (1cm) around the stone. Allow the glue to dry thoroughly.

With a double strand of waxed thread in a comfortable length (see Length of Thread on page 26), knot and stitch through the ultra-suede from the back (location 1), exiting as close to the edge of the stone as possible.

String six 11/0 seed beads and place along edge of stone, then stitch through the ultra-suede to the back (location 2).

Come up again between the third and fourth bead (location 3) and pass back through the last three beads.

String on three more beads. Stitch down through the ultra-suede (location 4) then come up just before the last set of three beads.

Repeat all the way around the stone.

Finish first row with even bead count

Adjust the bead count in the last stitch to ensure an even number of beads. Here, I'm adding four beads instead of three to make it an even number.

Start circular peyote

After the initial row of bead embroidery, come up through the ultra-suede and into the first bead. Start a circular peyote stitch by picking up one bead, passing over one from the base row, and stitching into the next.

Build up peyote base

Continue to stitch even-count circular peyote, making sure to step up at the end of each row. (To step up, pass the needle up into the first bead from the last row.) Build up the peyote bezel until you reach the top edge of the stone.

5

Stitch peyote decrease

When you come up to the top of the stone, you will need to decrease peyote to encapsulate the stone. You can decrease either by reducing the size of the beads in the next row, or by picking up one bead and passing through two beads from the previous row. (Reducing the bead number will create a deep 'V' that looks odd. However, on your next row, this 'V' will be filled in with one bead.)

When the stone is encapsulated and you like the look of the bezel, weave in all loose threads (see Weaving in a Tail on page 30).

6

Begin bead embroidery

Begin a new thread. Stitch a row of beads through the ultra-suede adjacent to the first row of the bezel in the same way you stitched the first row of the bezel (step 2).

Hint

For step 6, try using any size, or combination of sizes, of seed beads in the bead embroidery—asymmetry is OK! You may also include any accent beads or large seed beads.

7

Build up bead embroidery

Continue adding rows of bead embroidery until the overall piece is slightly larger than the size you want. Snip off the excess ultra-suede, making sure you don't cut into the thread. Set the bezel aside.

8

Prepare wire

Using your fingers, straighten the piece of 4" (10cm) 18-gauge wire.

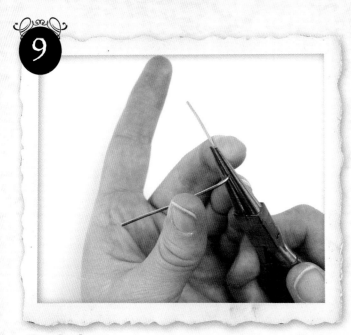

Bend wire

Using round-nose pliers, grasp the center of the wire piece and bend both ends toward each other, making it into a hairpin shape.

Close hairpin

Using the chain-nose pliers, gently squeeze the ends together so the hairpin is as tight as possible.

Make 'C'

Using the widest part of the round-nose pliers, wrap the hairpin end into a 'C' shape. The 'C' should be no longer than a third of the width of the bezel.

Cut ends

Using the flush-cut wire cutters, trim the ends of the wire so the clasp length is ½ the width of the bezel.

Bend ends to provide 'grab'

With round-nose pliers, slightly bend the clipped ends away from the 'C'. This will provide an anchor to help secure the clasp onto the bezel.

Sew clasp onto bezel

Place the clipped end against the bottom of the bezel (check that it faces the correct direction by laying the clasp, bezel and beadwork together). Press the anchor into the ultra-suede. Sew the clipped end to the ultra-suede to secure it to the bezel. Keep sewing until the clasp doesn't twist or move.

Hide clasp ends

Using scissors, cut a small slit into the middle of the second piece of ultra-suede just big enough to fit over the clasp. Glue the ultra-suede into place and set aside to dry.

Peyote extension

After the glue is completely dry, cut off the excess ultra-suede.

Build up a lip of beading on the back of the bezel. To do so, begin a new thread secured into the bezel and exiting a bead from the outer-most edge of the bead embroidery. Turn the bezel over and stitch a row of circular peyote with 11/0 seed beads.

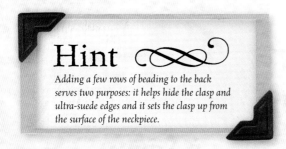

Hint ∾

Adding a few rows of beading to the back serves two purposes: it helps hide the clasp and ultra-suede edges and it sets the clasp up from the surface of the neckpiece.

Build up peyote extension

Stitch more rows of peyote. Keep adding rows until you are happy with the height, making sure it is not quite as high as the clasp. Weave in all loose thread (see Weaving in a Tail on page 30).

Attach loop

Start a new thread in the main piece. Sew the jump ring onto one end by passing the needle through the beads on the piece and sewing around the lower portion of the jump ring. (You can make your own jump ring with 18-gauge wire following the instructions on page 36.)

Attach bezel to piece

Verify orientation of the bezel clasp by laying it onto the end of the piece and lining it up with the jump ring sewn onto the opposite end. Attach the bezel by stitching back and forth through the beads on the piece and the beads on one edge of the clasp. Weave in the loose ends.

Join hook and loop

To close the piece, hook the clasp over the jump ring.

Freeform Color Flow

As the sun peeks over the horizon, the sky comes alive with colors moving seamlessly from yellow and orange through pink, purple and blue. Gazing into the depths of tropical waters, your eye is pulled from green to turquoise to blue to indigo. Roses glow as the intense inner color slowly transitions to pale outer petals. Moving from one color to another without sharp transitions is one of nature's successful color schemes and has been mimicked in Impressionist art, color-wash quilts and even garden borders. By wandering with color, you will create this glow in your beadwork.

The good news is that color flow can be achieved between any two colors! The key is in creating a smooth blend of beads that gradually moves from one color to the next so that it is difficult to tell where one color ends and the other begins. Monochromatic bead soups, with highlights and shadows (see page 20), will give you the basis for flowing between colors. These soups are already rich in texture and movement and are able to lean toward a myriad of other colors depending on the elements in the soup you choose to focus on.

Successful color flow is accomplished in three steps: making monochromatic bead soups with depth and movement; creating transitions between them; and stitching beads in a manner that hides the transitions between colors. These concepts are similar for all of the projects in this section—only the stitches and overall design differs from piece to piece. In *Wander With Color Necklace* (page 99), you will learn how to adapt color-flow techniques into the *Wandering Path Necklace* design (page 61). *Wander With Color Bracelet* (page 106) will show you how to use the color-flow techniques with freeform peyote. The gallery (page 108) will give you examples of how to incorporate color flow into any beadweaving design to create stunning pieces of beadwork that come alive with color.

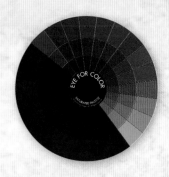

MATERIALS

basic beadweaving kit

numerous monochromatic seed bead soups, each at least 45 grams

gems in colors to complement seed bead soups

WANDER WITH COLOR NECKLACE

Colors glow in this variation of the *Wandering Path Necklace* (page 61), where movement in color is coupled with freeform netting to create artwork as fun to make as it is to wear. Choosing the color for your piece is enjoyable, but can be overwhelming. Look for inspiration in nature, a favorite piece of art or fabric, or pull out your color wheel and start laying colors side by side.

BEAD SOUP RECIPE:
Autumn Sunrise

An autumn sunrise off the deck of my parents' house, looking across Puget Sound to Mount Rainier, inspired the full spectrum of analogous colors in this necklace.

2

Choose monochromatic soups close on color wheel

Once you decide what colors you want in your project, then it is time to create bead soups for each of the color families. Refer to Creating Monochromatic Bead Soup (page 20) to create base soups full of rich shadows, highlights and variations in texture.

To make it easy on yourself, start by choosing two monochromatic bead soups that are close to each other. Close can simply mean two colors lying next to each other on the color wheel, as in the analogous blue to purple to pink soups shown here.

Choose monochromatic soups close in value and saturation

Colors can also be close if they are similar in saturation (how deep and intense the color) or value (how light or dark). Successful flow between the split complementary pair here is achieved because the pink and orange soups are both highly saturated.

Lay out bead soups

Pour small piles of each soup onto your bead mat in the order you envision them in your final piece. When you see the colors laid out, you may want to alter some piles or change the order. The best flow will be achieved between two bead soups that are closely related in some way (either on the color wheel, in value or in saturation).

4

Hint

You can move between colors more rapidly if you find actual transition pieces. Color-lined, metallic and AB beads have two or more colors within each bead and can act as fabulous transitions between two colors. This was helpful in the transition soup between the blue and brown bead soups after finding beads with both deep cobalt blue and a copper-brown color.

Create transition soups

Once you are happy with the general flow between all of your soups, it is time to create transitions. This is the key to seamlessly flowing from color to color. Transition soups are made by mixing a small amount of each original soup into a pile between them. Here, I have made transition soups between the orange and pink, pink and purple, purple and blue, and blue and brown.

5

Manipulate transition soup

If the transition soup looks speckled, you need to balance the colors in the soup. This can be achieved in several ways.

- Add multicolored beads, if possible, that contain colors of each of your main bead soup colors.
- Remove beads that lean too far away from a middle ground.
- Find transition beads that help blend hue, value and saturation.

Work with the transition soup until it is no longer speckled and looks like a true blend between the main soups.

6

Identify transition soups that are too far apart

If you can't get the transition soup to blend nicely, the initial soups may have been too far apart to flow together with just one step. The Dark Chocolate and Burnt Orange soups shown here are too far apart in value to blend seamlessly, so the transition soup is too speckled.

Create secondary transition soup

An additional transition soup is needed. In the darker soup (second from the left), I avoided adding the large bright orange beads because of their big impact (smaller beads are easier to blend because they take up less visual space).

Similarly, there aren't any of the dark brown 8/0 Hex beads in the soup next to the orange because they would have been too dramatic for blending. I also added more transition beads of rust to bring down the value of the chocolate soup and better link the brown and orange on the color wheel.

Occasionally, a soup not featured in the primary design can aid the transition. Here, I added a rust soup to level out the colors—you will hardly see it in the final piece, but it will give a smoother transition.

Add gems and other focal beads

Make up soups of gems, pearls and other treasures corresponding to each seed bead soup. You can keep them separated from the seed beads because they will be hand-stitched into your piece rather than placed in a freeform manner; throw them into the main soups to see how they look, but set them aside after that.

What you see on the bead mat at this point is a fair representation of the color flow you can achieve within the final piece, though how much you use of each soup will alter the effect.

Hint

Each of the soups (including the transition ones) should be large enough to use for the entire project. It is always better to have too much than too little. Leave some of each soup on the mat, but place most of each soup into its own container and number it so you remember the order. I use letters: A, B, etc., and a combination A/B to indicate the transition soup between A and B.

9

Lay out design

Define the overall design by laying out some of each bead soup on the bead mat. Manipulate the soup with your fingers until you like the design. Make notes or roughly sketch the design onto paper; if you have a camera, take a picture.

Take measurements of the overall length, adding however much you need for a closure, and note how much space you want for each color and each transition area.

10

String first row through all colors

With a double strand of waxed thread in a comfortable length (see Length of Thread on page 26), put on a stop bead (see Adding a Stop Bead on page 27), leaving a 4" (10cm) tail. String on the first row using the Stitching Techniques for Color Flow (see page 104), making sure each color segment is approximately the length you planned and you have a succession of color flows from the first bead soup to the last.

11

Second row of color blending

Turn the corner by passing through approximately the eighth bead from the end. Stitch the first 5" (13cm) in Modified 3-Bead Netting (see page 63) to reinforce the back of the necklace. Move to freeform netting in the middle of the necklace. Note that I am pulling some of the pink beads into the orange to diffuse the transition.

Hint

This project is freeform and organic: it can evolve, change shape and grow as you work. You may very well change your mind as you work and your piece takes on a life of its own. Many of my projects end up very different from my original design! Just make sure you are happy with the color progression in the bead soups.

Stitching Techniques for Color Flow

Use these stitching tricks to achieve smooth transitions between colors, as shown below for moving between the orange and pink soups, including the transition soup between them. The techniques for color flow are the same no matter which stitch you use and whether you are adding groups of beads at a time (as in freeform netting), or just one (as in freeform peyote).

It is important to stitch in a direction along the flow of color, rather than perpendicular to it. For instance, if you want the color to transition along the length of your piece, you need to do vertical stitching—set your length on the first row and build up width with each additional row.

Blend from bead soup A to transition soup A/B

String on a random assortment of beads from bead soup A to the length you would like for that color. As you approach the transition soup A/B from soup A, dip the needle into A, then grab a couple of beads from soup A/B. You can handpick these first transition beads so that they are close to the colors in A yet lean towards the color you are blending into (soup B).

Go back to a few beads from soup A then back again into the transition beads A/B. You should gradually work into the transition soup and start to incorporate ones that are closer to the colors in B.

If your transition mix looks speckled, remember to choose beads that lean toward both colors, and perhaps smaller beads, which tend to be a little easier to blend.

You should now be entirely in the transition soup A/B.

Blend from transition Soup A/B to bead soup B

While still in the transition soup A/B, begin adding beads that lean to B. Grab a few transition beads A/B and a couple of B beads.

Next, add more beads from B with just a few transition beads A/B that are close to the colors in B.

Finally, move entirely into B. This completes your first transition.

Hint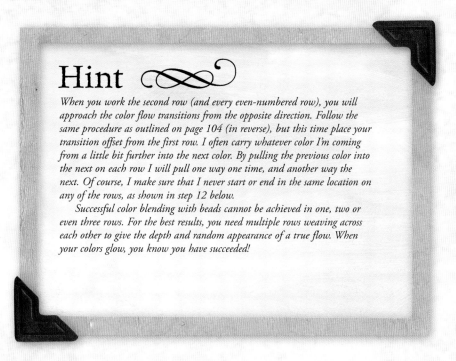

When you work the second row (and every even-numbered row), you will approach the color flow transitions from the opposite direction. Follow the same procedure as outlined on page 104 (in reverse), but this time place your transition offset from the first row. I often carry whatever color I'm coming from a little bit further into the next color. By pulling the previous color into the next on each row I will pull one way one time, and another way the next. Of course, I make sure that I never start or end in the same location on any of the rows, as shown in step 12 below.

Successful color blending with beads cannot be achieved in one, two or even three rows. For the best results, you need multiple rows weaving across each other to give the depth and random appearance of a true flow. When your colors glow, you know you have succeeded!

Build up rows

Build up the rows of the necklace, stitching the first and last 5" (13cm) in Modified 3-Bead Netting and stitching freeform netting in the middle of the necklace. Continue to blend colors from one soup to the next.

Add gems

As you add gems and pearls, you will find ones that act as transition pieces—pearls are wonderful for this. Keep building up rows until you have eliminated sharp transition lines and speckled areas.

When you are happy with the overall piece, weave in all loose threads (see Weaving in a Thread on page 30). Attach a closure (see pages 32–35).

Hint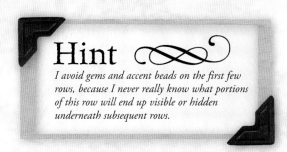

I avoid gems and accent beads on the first few rows, because I never really know what portions of this row will end up visible or hidden underneath subsequent rows.

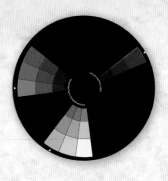

MATERIALS

basic beadweaving kit

numerous monochromatic bead soups, each at least 45 grams

gem soups in colors to complement bead soups

WANDER WITH COLOR BRACELET

Use freeform peyote stitches with color flow techniques to create an organic bracelet with texture, depth and movement. But don't limit yourself! I tucked a piece of beach glass into this bracelet using the beachcomber techniques on pages 74–76. You could also add fibers or a bezel!

BEAD SOUP RECIPE:

Earth Tones

Fort Warden, built in 1898 to protect the inner waters of Washington State, is located at the mouth of Puget Sound. Now the officers' quarters, mess hall and barracks are home to numerous festivals and art retreats, such as ArtFest held each year in early spring. While the classrooms and expansive lawns teem with creative energy, those in-the-know wander up into the old gun batteries on the hill with their cameras. Everywhere you turn, you will find old painted, then rusted, then repainted doors that enliven the grey concrete tunnels with unsaturated, earthy tones from the inner rings of the color wheel.

Lay out design

Lay out bead soups, transition soups and gem soups onto your bead mat in the order you envision them in your final piece and manipulate into your final design as you did for the *Wander With Color Necklace* (page 99). Take pictures, make sketches and take measurements for each segment of color. Number the bead soups and transition soups for future reference.

Complete first row

With a double strand of waxed thread in a comfortable length (see Length of Thread on page 26), put on a stop bead (see Adding a Stop Bead on page 24), leaving a 4" (10cm) tail. String on a random assortment of beads from each bead soup and transition soup to the length determined above. As you continue stringing on beads, use the Stitching Techniques for Color Flow as discussed on page 104.

Turn the corner by adding one bead, passing over the last bead from the first row and stitching into the next, just as in normal peyote.

Build up rows

Continue adding approximately one bead, passing over one and stitching into the next to build up the rows. Note that sometimes more than one bead will fit into a stitch. Make sure to follow the color blending techniques discussed on page 104, and carry each color a little into the next to further the random feel of the flow between colors.

Crunch bracelet

Build up the width with subsequent rows, and where the piece bends and buckles, fill the spaces in with gems. To enhance the texture and movement of the bracelet, scrunch it and fill in the cavities with more gems and strands of beads, some of which will act as transition pieces.

Keep building up rows until you have achieved the desired width and you have eliminated sharp color transition lines.

Weave in all loose threads (see Weaving in a Tail on page 30). Attach a closure (see pages 32–35).

Legacy—a tribute to Richard Gilbert

My father-in-law died suddenly on Father's Day 2004 in
the fields of his Oregon farm while my husband, two
little boys and I were picnicking unaware on our beach.
Working with beads helped me cope with my sorrow and
the family upheaval when my husband moved to Oregon
to help farm for the rest of the season.

The bead soups in this piece capture the colors of that
fateful day—red clay in the hills around the farm, rich
brown soil and lush green crops of the Willamette Valley,
and blue waters of Puget Sound. This necklace is a tribute
to Richard Gilbert, and though he is gone, his legacy of
hard work, high integrity and loving warmth lives on in
his 22 descendents. Techniques from all chapters come
together into the beadwork that radiates from the turquoise doughnut and weaves around and through the 22
treasures symbolizing each of his descendents.

Undersea Volcano

Molten lava flows out of an undersea volcano extinguishing life on tropical islands like Hunga Ha 'apai. Yet out of the devastation, new life emerges in a never-ending cycle.

This necklace is made using *Wanderlust Neckpiece* stitched in peyote and color flow techniques.

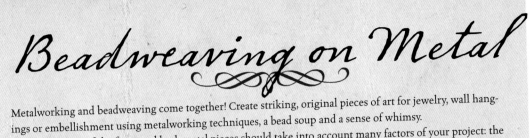

Beadweaving on Metal

Metalworking and beadweaving come together! Create striking, original pieces of art for jewelry, wall hangings or embellishment using metalworking techniques, a bead soup and a sense of whimsy.

The designs of the front and back metal pieces should take into account many factors of your project: the size and shape, what bead soup you want to use, and whether your metal will be a plain background or play more of a focal role in the overall look of your piece.

You may choose your metal first and create a bead soup to complement it, or vice versa. Perhaps you have a poem or an inspirational quote you want to stamp on the back, and your material and color choice will be designed around it—the combinations are endless.

The techniques in *Beads on Metal Simple Pendant* (page 112) are the jumping off point for a vast array of pieces. Variations of the design are endless. Your pieces can multiply for the *Moveable Connections Bracelet* (see page 124), stand alone as a broach, or make a bold statement, as with the *On and On Pendant* (page 122).

Metal and Wireworking Materials and Tools

Most of these tools and materials are inexpensive and readily available—though in some cases, I recommend spending more money to get a better quality. Create this basic metalworking kit to have on hand as you create.

Basic Metalworking Kit

Sheet Metal

Pieces of 24-gauge metal are used for the front and back of these projects. Copper, sterling silver and aluminum are easy to cut and stamp. Brass is a little less malleable, but very beautiful to work with. Note that aluminum, though very easy to work with, is difficult to colorize and antique.

Metal Shears

Ones with smooth blades specifically designed for jewelry making are much easier to use than those you can buy in the hardware store. The hardware variety has a serrated edge that you must meticulously file off and the blades are designed to peel the edges apart (like a banana), which is difficult to flatten after cutting.

Metal File

You can find these in any hardware store. Use them to smooth the edges of the cut sheet metal to make your pieces safer to work with and wear.

Metal Hole Punch

Small, portable and very useful, this is one cool tool! It makes riveting and adding jump rings to metal pieces a breeze. You can also use a drill press or a hand-held rotary tool in place of a hole punch.

Ball-Peen Hammer

The hardware variety works great. I like to have 4 ounce (113g) and 8 ounce (227g) ones on hand for various purposes.

Bench Block

I like the flat steel blocks (rather than anvils) for metalworking. I use one side for all my metalworking, peening, stamping and other actions that will mar the surface of the block. The other side I reserve for wire working so the surface remains smooth.

Rawhide or Plastic Mallet

Use to flatten the metal sheet when it curls as you work harden it. These mallets won't leave marks like a hammer does.

Decorative and Alpha-numeric Metal Stamps

These are a must if you want to include words or decorations or to date your piece.

Antiquing Solution

I like using Liver of Sulfur in crystal form but take extra care to keep it sealed from moisture when not in use. I keep a plastic container with a lid specifically for antiquing along with some plastic forks to help agitate the solution. Very small bits of crystal are mixed with hot water for each batch, so a container of Liver of Sulfur will go a long way. Follow manufacturer instructions for mixing and disposal.

Steel Wool

Pick up a bag of 000 steel wool at the hardware store. It is great for taking off the bulk of the blackened surface after antiquing, while still leaving the stamped impressions dark.

Polishing Cloth (optional)

An inexpensive, portable and effective way to polish your piece after it has been antiqued. Use if you want to buff the surface back to the bare metal color, while leaving the stamped impressions dark.

Permanent Felt Pen and Ruler

Use these for designing your piece and marking where to cut the metal.

Cellophane Tape

Tape helps keep the metal pieces from moving around when punching holes with the metal hole punch.

Basic Wireworking Kit

Basic wireworking materials and tools are all you need. See if you have any of the following items in your workspace before purchasing them.

Wires

24- to 22-gauge wire in the same colors as the sheet metal you choose to use in a project.

16- to 18-gauge wire for making jump rings. You can also purchase jump rings if you don't want to make them.

14-gauge wire for making rivets.

Pliers

Inexpensive round-nose and chain-nose pliers are OK for these projects.

Flush-Cut Wire Cutters

Spend a bit extra to get good quality flush-cut wire cutters. You need a very flat cut when making rivets.

Chasing Hammer

This will be used only if you make jump rings, so if you purchase jump rings already made then you don't need this tool.

Beadweaving tools

The beadweaving materials are similar to those needed in all of the prior projects:

Basic beadweaving kit (see page 24); seed bead soup, small accent beads in colors to complement the seed bead soup, and medium to large focal beads for center of beadwork (optional).

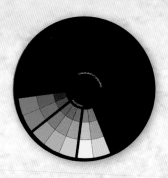

MATERIALS

basic beadweaving kit

basic metalworking kit

basic wireworking kit

30 grams seed bead soup plus a handful of gems to complement colors in soup

BEADS ON METAL SIMPLE PENDANT

Freeform beadweaving can be incorporated into even the most rigid of structures. Wire anchors allow you to add beadwork, while a backing piece pulls double duty by hiding the anchors and providing a surface for poetry or other inspirations.

I like to derive inspiration from the bead soup I've chosen and stamp a poem, thoughts or random words on the back metal. You may also just stamp out your name and date or decorative markings. Anything goes!

BEAD SOUP RECIPE:

The Grass is Greener

Our vacation property on Whidbey Island is in a wetland buffer zone, so we are required to keep it all natural—no lawns, no flower beds, no gardens. Just long grasses, reeds, native shrubs and lots of birds, frogs and deer.

A few hundred feet from us are folks who built before the wetland restrictions, and yes, their manicured lawns are greener, but ours is a beautiful expanded monochromatic palette with shadows, highlights, dark and light green, shades of blue and yellow and brown—so full of life and interest.

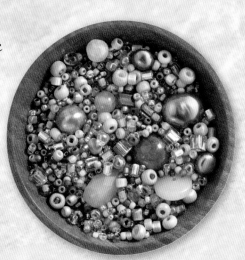

1

Choose materials

You may decide to choose your metal first and create a bead soup to complement it or vice versa.

Start by making a pile of your bead soup on the metal and stand back to see the effect.

2

Hint ∽

Don't feel limited to keep to symmetry and squares—cutting corners slightly off angle can add interest.

Cut front and back metal

Using the metal shears, cut the front and back pieces to the shape you want. Here, I used a permanent black marker to draw the shapes I wanted first.

3

File edges

Using a metal file, smooth the edges and corners until they are smooth to the touch.

Hint ∽

Metal files have a nap—just like a cheese grater. Hold the metal piece in your non-dominant hand and file away from you. Flip the piece to file in the opposite direction.

4

Flatten metal

Flatten the metal with light taps of a rawhide hammer on the bench block. The rawhide hammer is soft enough to flatten the metal without marking it.

Hint ∽

Use a permanent marker to label both sides of the bench block—one side for stamping, one side for finishing. It will save you from surprise indents in your finished work.

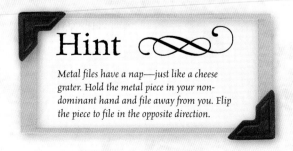

Stamp onto metal

Place the metal on the bench block. Hold the stamp straight and place it directly onto metal. Using the ball-peen hammer, hit the end of the stamp with one sharp rap.

If the back metal is visible from the front in your design, make sure the stamping on the back doesn't show through on these exposed areas.

Decorate edges of face metal

You can leave the edges plain or embellish them with metal stamps or with your ball-peen hammer. Since beadwork will cover most of my piece, I have chosen to just lightly peen the edges of the face metal.

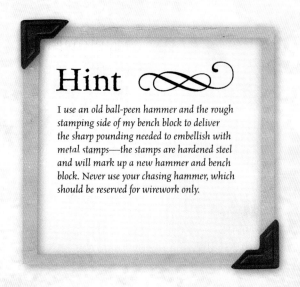

Hint

I use an old ball-peen hammer and the rough stamping side of my bench block to deliver the sharp pounding needed to embellish with metal stamps—the stamps are hardened steel and will mark up a new hammer and bench block. Never use your chasing hammer, which should be reserved for wirework only.

Decorate edges of back metal

On my piece, the slightly larger back metal forms a frame around the front metal. Therefore, embellishments in the frame area need to be applied to the opposite side of the back metal. Before you decorate the frame, sandwich the metal together and note which side of the back metal you need to decorate to have it show up nicely on the front of your piece.

I have peened the edges and am adding a dotted edge design using the "period" from my alpha-numeric metal stamps.

Hint

Your metal sheet will curl when you work harden it with stamping, so you will need to periodically hammer it back into shape with a rawhide or plastic mallet.

Don't be shy about asymmetry—balance doesn't have to be symmetrical and can be more interesting when it's not!

9

Lay out bead soup design

Place the front and back metal pieces together. With your face metal right side up, pour some of your bead soup into the center. With your fingers, move the beads around on the metal until you come up with a pleasing design. Don't forget to place your accent bead on top for an idea of where it will look best.

With the permanent felt pen, mark a set of two dots at each of the outside points on your design. Your beadwork will be contained within the boundaries of these points.

Use each anchor as set of points

Your design must have at least three anchors (of two dots each) where you plan to attach the beadwork.

When you have finished designing with the bead soup, scoop it up and set it aside.

10

Hint

The goal is to provide small loops on top of the face metal so the needle can pass through while you are adding beads. The loops shouldn't be so large that they show once the beadwork is in place. You also want to avoid large bulges on the backside.

Punch holes for anchors

Punch small holes at each of the marked points with the metal punch.

Place wire anchors

Thread the 22- to 24-gauge wire between an anchor set so the exposed wire on the front of the face metal is between points of the same set. The wire should be long enough to pass between each set on the back of the face metal.

Hint

It is best to avoid placing beadwork close to the corners of the face metal so you will have room to rivet, as explained later.

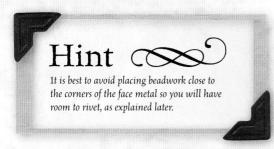

12

Shape anchors

Use your fingers to gently coax the wire to create small wire mounds on the front of the face metal. Guide the wire so it lies flat on the back.

13

Cut wire on back

Weave the wire through all the anchor points. Twist the ends of the wire together on the back of the face metal. Using the flush-cut wire cutter, cut the wire so it doesn't extend beyond the edge of the face metal. Press the wire flat into the center of the back.

14

Hint

To hide the anchor wire between the metal pieces, it may be necessary to gently bend the edges of the metal into the center of the "sandwich."

Mark for rivets

Sandwich the metal pieces together, making sure the correct sides are facing out and they are oriented in the right direction. Wrap a piece of cellophane tape around the center to hold the metal pieces together. Mark locations for each rivet with the permanent felt marker.

To secure the metal pieces together and adequately hide the anchor wire, you will need to rivet in at least three, preferably four, places.

15

Punch hole for rivet

Make a hole using the small end of the metal punch. Choose wire in a gauge that is the same size as the hole punch—you don't want it so small that it slips through and bends easily. Here, the small end of the metal punch is the same size as 14-gauge wire.

Hint

Rivet each hole in place (see steps 17–18) before punching the next so there is less risk of the pieces slipping and the holes not matching up.

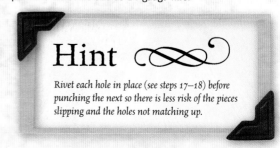

16

Cut wire for rivet

Insert a short piece of wire through the hole in both sheets. Flush cut both ends of the wire approximately ⅛"–³⁄₁₆" (3mm–5mm), or just long enough to go through both pieces of metal with excess to pound into a rivet.

17

Hint ⚬⚬

I hold my piece slightly above the bench block so the wire emerges on either side of the metal.

Set rivet with ball-peen hammer

Place the corner you need to rivet on the bench block, position the metal so it sticks out both sides and pound gently it with your ball-peen hammer into the center of the wire. Use light taps (not like the "sharp rap" from step 5) so you don't bend your wire.

18

Flip to set rivet

Once you have widened out the wire enough so it won't fall through the hole, turn the work over and gently pound on the other side. Keep flipping over and pounding out the rivet until it is flush with the metal sheet and has widened enough to secure the pieces together. Repeat steps 15–18 for the remaining three rivets.

19

Antique metal (optional)

Remove the tape.

If you embellish the metal and want the stamping and peening to really stand out, use Liver of Sulfur (following the manufacturer's directions) to darken the impressions.

Sand to reveal stamping (optional)

Using 000 steel wool, remove antiqued surface from the metal to reveal stamp designs. You can take the surface back to the original metal or leave it slightly antiqued, as I did in this piece.

Add beadwork

With a double strand of waxed thread in a comfortable length (see Length of Thread on page 26), put on a stop bead (see Adding a Stop Bead on page 27), leaving a 4" (10cm) tail. String on a random mix of beads. The length should be slightly longer than the distance between two sets of anchors. Pass the needle under the wire at the first anchor.

Start second row

Turn the corner by adding approximately five beads and stitching through a bead from your first row. This bead is the first shared bead for rows 1 and 2.

Adjust the tension to remove gaps and any exposed thread, especially near the wire. You will now have a loop of beads around the wire.

Complete second row

Add beads at random and stitch into the first row wherever the end of the added strand falls. Work all the way to the second anchor in this freeform style.

Pass into a bead from the first row that lies just in front of the second anchor. Pull off the stop bead and any excess beads from row 1.

Secure end to anchor

Adjust the tension to avoid any gaps or exposed thread; tie the working thread and tail together to maintain the tension. (Leave the tail so you can weave it into your beadwork later.) Pass the needle under the second anchor.

Turn corner

Add approximately five beads and pass into a bead from either the first or second row. Freeform stitch back to the first anchor. Pass under the wire with the needle.

Repeat for all anchors

Work at least three rows between the first two anchors. Pass under each wire a couple of times to secure the beadwork; maintain the tension at all times to avoid exposed thread.

Repeat steps 22-26 to add beading to the remaining two anchors.

27. Add focal beads

Once you have beadwork between each of the anchors, you can start adding gems. Come out of any bead in the beadwork in the general area where you would like to add the large focal bead. Place the focal bead in the desired spot on the piece and stitch into it. If needed, add beads to hide the thread before you stitch into the focal bead.

Add more beads as needed to hide the thread and stitch back into the anchor strands to secure the focal bead.

28. Build up until complete

Fill in with more freeform stitches, adding more gems and beads, until you are happy with the overall look. When you are finished, tie a half hitch around the working thread. Weave in all loose threads (see Weaving in a Tail on page 30).

To hang the pendant, punch a hole in the metal at the top of the piece and add a jump ring (see Making Jump Rings on page 36).

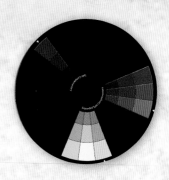

MATERIALS

basic beadweaving kit

basic metalworking kit

basic wireworking kit

ruler

30 grams seed bead soup plus a handful of small gems to complement colors in soup

OUT OF BOUNDS

For fun, try making the front and back metal completely different shapes. The only requirement is that the back metal hides the anchor wire. There are no boundaries!

BEAD SOUP RECIPE:

Antique Brass

Piles of old brass coins, lapis and old glass bring to mind another era, another century of trade in Asia. This rich, earthy palette lies in the inner circle of the color wheel with blue and gold—two parts of a split complementary. You could always add the earthy orange of carnelian, bauxite or old coral to complete the harmony and provide a bright splash of color to the palette.

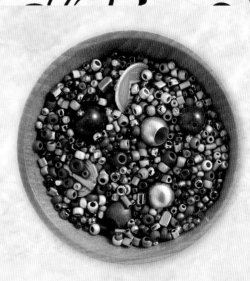

Design piece and cut metal

Cut and file the edges of the front metal following steps 1-3 on page 113.

Decorate face metal

Decorate the metal with stamps and your hammer as desired. (For this piece, I decided to peen a large portion of the face metal.)

Flatten metal

Using the rawhide hammer, flatten the piece if it curls up.

Define region covered by face metal

Place the backing metal on top of the front metal. Using the ruler and permanent felt marker, draw an outline of the back metal.

Stamp within outline

Using stamps of your choosing, decorate the back metal. Stamp within the outline so the stamping on the back won't show on the front.

Finish the piece by following steps 8-28 on pages 115-119.

MATERIALS

basic beadweaving kit

basic metalworking kit

basic wireworking kit

30 grams seed bead soup plus a handful of gems to complement colors in soup

accent gems of uniform size to separate beaded drops

ON AND ON PENDANT

Your beadwork doesn't need to be confined within the boundaries set by the anchors in the metal. These delicate drops of beadwork can be added onto a simple pendant at any time.

BEAD SOUP RECIPE:

Golden Raspberry

Every now and then, a really scrumptious bead pops up and inspires a whole new palette. These tiny charlottes have an AB (Aurora Borealis) finish, making them shine in deep raspberry pink, gold and bronze. I expanded on each of the color families to create a rich, regal mix. Note that the color relationship is two parts of a tetrad with golds from the inner ring of the color wheel.

Add onto beadwork

Follow the steps for Beads on Metal Simple Pendant (see pages 112–119) to create the base for this pendant.

Begin a new thread (see Beginning and Ending Threads in a Project on page 28) and weave through the beads in the piece to where you would like to add more beadwork.

String on the decorative gem, then a random assortment of beads from your bead soup until the strand is long enough to form a loop. The size of the loop will depend on how large you want the added beadwork to be.

Secure the loop by passing back through the decorative gem and into some beads in the previous beadwork. Keep good tension so there is no exposed thread.

Build up bead loop

Weave around the beads in the main piece, and thread back through the gem. Build up the beaded drop with freeform stitches inside the loop.

Continue as desired

Continue building up the stitches until the drop is filled in. You can add as many drops as desired in the same manner.

When you are satisfied with the design, weave in all loose threads (see Weaving in a Tail on page 30).

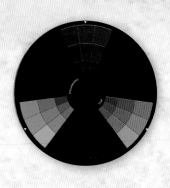

MATERIALS

basic beadweaving kit

basic metalworking kit

basic wireworking kit

30 grams seed bead soup

4mm to 7mm gems for the center of each bracelet component

large hook-and-eye clasp

MOVEABLE
CONNECTIONS BRACELET

This bracelet is composed of several simple Beads on Metal pendants connected with jump rings to allow movement and draping.

The project will flow more smoothly if all of the metal work is completed first. Measure and cut out all the back and face metal pieces at one time. Then stamp your desired design (I added a poem) on the bracelet components and finish the edges. Follow the instructions for the *Beads on Metal Simple Pendant* to finish each component.

BEAD SOUP RECIPE:

Harvest

I remember driving through Napa Valley in the early 1970s on our way down the coast to my Aunt Carolyn's house in the Bay area. Dad brought a case of his homemade wine to trade with the little family run wineries that dotted our path. Not many visitors back then—we were treated to special wine tasting with the owners and I would drink in the smells of fermenting grapes, watch wine swirl in the glasses and listen to my dad swap stories with the entrepreneurs of California wine. Cheers!

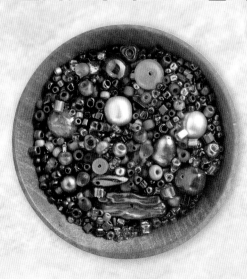

Prepare individual links

Follow steps 1–20 on pages 113–118 to prepare the individual links. Lay them out in order. Place a small sticky note tab on each to mark the order and top of the piece so any writing on the back flows from left to right.

Mark jump ring placement

Lay out the components face up and in order. Using the permanent marker, mark where the hole for the jump rings should be.

Punch holes

Punch holes with a larger bit than the diameter of the jump ring wire to allow movement in the joint—I use the "black" side of my hole punch. Unless you choose to solder the jump rings, I advise using two between each component for stability as well as balance.

Finish bracelet

If desired, all of the components and the jump rings can be dipped in Liver of Sulfur to darken the impressions and antique the surface of the metal. Polish to the extent you would like and then you are ready to add the beadwork.

Following steps 21–28 on pages 118–119 and using your bead soup and accent beads, embellish each of the components.

Make the needed number of jump rings (see Making Jump Rings on page 36). Attach each completed component with the jump rings. To the end components, add the hook-and-eye clasp.

Hint

Make sure to open and close jump rings in a scissor fashion to maintain the shape of the jump ring.

Resources

There are many online resources for seed beads and jewelry supplies—too numerous for me to list. I really enjoy going to local bead shops and craft stores to see the beads up close. It's exhilarating to mix-and-match seed bead colors, textures, shapes and sizes when the mood strikes. Visit your local craft store and bead shops for some instant color gratification!

Here are a few of my favorite, books and other resources. I hope they inspire you as much as they have inspired me.

Beverly Ash Gilbert
www.gilbertdesigns.net
seed bead and gem soups, *Eye For Color* color wheel system

Theo Chocolate
www.theochocolate.com
chocolate bars, chocolate confections, sipping chocolate and so much more

My Favorite Books on Color

Color Confidence for Quilters, Beyer, Jinny. Quilt Digest Press, 1992.

The Gardener's Palette, Creating Color in the Garden. Eddison, Sydney. Contemporary Books, 2003.

Tricia Guild on Colour. Guild, Tricia. Conran Octopus Ltd, 1992.

Inspiration. Guild, Tricia, Elspeth Thompson, and James Merrell. Quadrille Publishing Ltd, 2006

Color Me Beautiful. Jackson, Carole. Acropolis Books, 1980.

Watercolor Quilts. Magaret, P. M. & Slusser, D. I. That Patchwork Place, 1993.

Color Works, The Crafter's Guide to Color. Menz, Deb. Interweave Press, 2004.

A Passion for Flowers. Roehm, Carolyn. HarperCollins, 1997.

Great Resources on Techniques

The Art & Elegance of Beadweaving: New Jewelry Designs with Classic Stitches. Wells, Carol Wilcox. Lark Books, 2002.

All Wired Up. Lareau, Mark. Interweave Press, 2000.

Tracy Stanley, classes in wire and metal work (wiredarts.net). If you haven't had a class from Tracy, treat yourself the next time she's in town!

NanC Meinhardt, classes in freeform beadweaving (www.nancmeinhardt.com). A freeform diva and bead soup queen!

Index

Find more inspiration with these books

Beyond Beading Basics

by Carole Rodgers

Take your beading skills to the next level as you go Beyond Beading Basics. Conquer the more complex aspects of beading, such as using common bead findings as integral parts of your designs, using multiple-hole beads, making baskets and other shapes with wire and beads and how to combine stitches to achieve unique effects. Carole Rodgers offers you more than twenty-five projects and an equal number of techniques to launch you into bead artistry.

ISBN-10: 0-89689-925-X
ISBN-13: 978-0-89689-925-4
paperback, 144 pages, Z3628

The Beader's Bible

by Dorothy Wood

This indispensable guide to beads and beading techniques, provides essential know-how together with a wide range of inspirational projects, tips and ideas. Each chapter focuses on a different beading technique, guiding you through basic skills, tools and materials, before moving on to over thirty step-by-step projects, ranging from beautiful bags and jewelry to stylish scarves and accessories.

ISBN 10: 0-7153-2300-8
ISBN 13: 978-0-7153-2300-7
paperback with flaps, 160 pages, Z2314

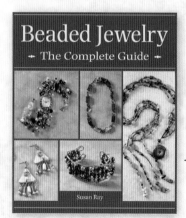

Beaded Jewelry: The Complete Guide

by Susan Ray

Jewelry and beading expert Susan Ray, along with dozens of expert jewelry artists, bring you this complete tutorial for making your own jewelry to fit your personal style. Whether you prefer professional and polished, classic and elegant, or casual and comfortable, you will find the designs and information needed to complete your jewelry pieces using this book.

ISBN 10: 0-89689-385-5
ISBN 13: 978-0-89689-385-6
hard cover with encased spiral, 256 pages, Z0105